PROPERTY SERIES

Buy-to-Let
Bible

Ajay Ahuja

Buy-to-Let Bible
by Ajay Ahuja

1st edition 2002
2nd edition 2003
   Reprinted twice
   Reprinted 2004
3rd edition 2005
   Reprinted 2005
   Reprinted 2006
4th edition 2008

© 2008 Lawpack Publishing

Lawpack Publishing Limited
76–89 Alscot Road
London SE1 3AW

www.lawpack.co.uk

ISBN: 978-1-905261-70-3

Exclusion of Liability and Disclaimer

While every effort has been made to ensure that this Lawpack publication provides accurate and expert guidance, it is impossible to predict all the circumstances in which it may be used. Accordingly, neither the publisher, author, retailer, nor any other suppliers shall be liable to any person or entity with respect to any loss or damage caused or alleged to be caused by the information contained in or omitted from this Lawpack publication.

For convenience (and for no other reason) 'him', 'he' and 'his' have been used throughout and should be read to include 'her', 'she' and 'her'.

Contents

List of figures

List of tables

I dedicate this book to my mother.

Thanks to Anjana and Tom for their comments.
A special thanks to Ellie for her support and research.

About the author

Ajay Ahuja has been investing in property since 1996. He personally owns a portfolio of 200 properties worth £13.6m and has helped over 500 people invest in exactly the same sort of properties he has invested in.

All in all, he has sourced over 1,000 cash flow positive properties for clients in the UK and USA and he has helped clients build a healthy current income. He has even helped people leave their nine-to-five jobs and go on to be prolific professional property investors.

You can find out all about what Ajay has to offer at www.ahuja.co.uk.

Introduction

I started virtually with nothing. I bought my first property when I was 24 with £500 and now, at the age of 35, I own 200 properties worth over £13 million and I earn an income in excess of £500,000 per annum. It's not difficult but it requires DEDICATION, PERSISTENCE and DISCIPLINE. If you lack any of the above, then forget it.

My dedication, persistence and discipline about being rich were not driven by money but by freedom – the freedom to do what I like, when I like, without worrying about my boss or my wallet. Freedom doesn't have to be your driving factor; it could be a brand new Ferrari or private schooling for your children. Whatever it is, it's this that will keep you going. With the right properties, financial products and tenants, there is no doubt you'll succeed, and this book will show you how to go about finding the right properties, financial products, tenants and more.

So why choose property? Why not invest in stocks and shares? The first reason is that property carries an inherently low risk factor. Houses will not go out of fashion or become obsolete like services or products. They are an essential for us all. That's why house prices have consistently doubled every 10–15 years over the last century. Coupled with the fact that monthly rental values rise with wages (which is a function of inflation) and that the mortgage payment is relatively fixed (only altering with interest rate fluctuations), the profit element always rises. In addition, after the bills have been paid, the rent is all profit. That's why many people see investing in property as their pension fund.

The second reason is basic economics. With an expanding population, fragmenting families, an increasingly mobile workforce, fewer properties for sale and fewer council owned properties, THE DEMAND FOR RENTAL PROPERTIES EXCEEDS SUPPLY.

The third reason is an inherent attribute in all of us – we're lazy! To play the stock market properly requires lengthy research, ongoing monitoring and nerves of steel for the duration of the investment. That's why three out of four private investors lose money. When a property is set up properly, you just sit back and watch the money roll in.

I am a chartered accountant. I left employment when I was 27 to get into the property business and I must admit the training I received in accountancy and, more importantly, in business has helped me in my success. However, the principles involved are not difficult to grasp. I bought my first property in 1996 for myself to live in, couldn't get used to it, and so let it out. I soon realised that the tenant was paying my mortgage as well as my beer money (about £120 per month), and it required minimal effort from me. I thought, 'This is easy!' so I bought another one and did the same. 198 properties later…you get the idea.

So whether you're thinking of creating a multi-million-pound property empire or simply buying the house next door to earn a modest secondary income, this book is for you. But before you get pound signs in your eyes you have to ask yourself: Is property right for you? There are four key questions you have to ask yourself:

1. Can I budget well?

2. Do I like and am I capable of dealing with people from a range of backgrounds?

3. Do I like property?

4. Am I a responsible person?

Can I budget well?

Are you the type of person who spends his wages before they are earned? Do you often use your overdraft facility and credit cards to fund your lifestyle? Do you make impulse purchases on the high street and then regret them later? Do you wake up in the morning after an evening out and wonder how you managed to spend all of the £100 that was in your pocket the night before? If this sounds familiar, then investing in property is currently not for you. Investing in property could be an option at a later date but your spending has to mature. A mortgage is a legal commitment to pay a sum of money on regular set dates and a breach of this commitment can result in damage to your credit rating and it could ultimately lead to bankruptcy.

Sometimes rent from several properties comes in cash on the same day. I might have £3,000 in cash in my pocket and it certainly gives you a feeling that you're £3,000 richer, but you're not! You've got to pay the mortgage, service charges, building insurance, etc. You have to be disciplined enough to bank the cash and not assume that all the rent is profit, which is surprisingly easy to forget.

Do I like and am I capable of dealing with people from a range of backgrounds?

The type of people you'll be meeting with will be:

- **Tenants:** They can be of any age over 18, from any profession, male or female, from any race or religion. Have you got any hang-ups about a certain group of people?

- **Estate and letting agents:** Despite what people say about agents, my experience with them is that they conduct themselves in a professional manner. They can be a bit pushy sometimes, but you've got to expect that when dealing with people whose business depends on the sale or management of an asset worth many thousands of pounds. Are you easily persuaded? Can you stand your ground?

- **Solicitors:** Usually very intelligent people. Can you convince him of your intelligence so that he doesn't keep you in the dark when you want to know what's going on?

- **Lenders:** Your point of contact is normally a call centre operator. Are you able to keep your cool to extract the right information from the operator?

- **Mortgage brokers:** Again, very sharp people. Can you keep up with his calculations? Are you asking the right questions?

Do I like property?

There is absolutely no point in getting involved in property if you're not interested in property. Any successful businessman will tell you that if you're thinking of starting a business, the first thing you've got to ask yourself is if you enjoy the business you're getting into. Do you believe in the product? Is the business you are contemplating something that your mind naturally wanders to? Is the line between work and pleasure blurred when it comes to looking at and maintaining property?

It's your interest in property that will ensure that you dedicate the correct amount of time in order for your property business to succeed.

Am I a responsible person?

You have many legal obligations to your tenant, lender and letting agent. Property is a serious business. You have to be aware of these obligations and be prepared to fulfil them. Failure to do so can have serious repercussions, including jail!

Well, is property for you?

If you can answer 'Yes' to three out of four of those questions, then you're basically ready for property investment. To be really good, though, you need to work on the question you answered 'No' to. If you answered 'Yes' to all questions, then there is nothing to stop you from becoming a millionaire within the next 10 years, and that is fact. The most common type of business in the last 50 years that made people millionaires is either commercial or residential property.

The formula

The formula detailed below is the formula that has made me a millionaire. The same formula has created many millionaires – it's nothing groundbreaking or original. Property is inherently a long-term path to wealth – that is the nature of property. If you have the patience to play the property market, you'll make money. I have to admit that my rapid acquisition in wealth is partly due to the property boom since 1996, but it's also adhering to the principles I stuck to, detailed in this book.

The formula is simple

- **Find the initial investment:** Starting a business requires some initial capital, but getting into the property game isn't as expensive as you may think. It's possible to start with nothing! Chapter 1 deals with how you can identify your attitude to risk and it provides inventive ways of how you can raise your initial investment so you can purchase your first property. Once you've raised the initial investment, you can progress to finding the right lender to finance the property you wish to buy.

- **Find the right lender:** In chapter 2 you'll create a profile most suited to your personal circumstances and attitudes in order to find the right lender for you.

- **Find the right property:** From chapter 3 you'll be able to identify easily properties that can give you a significant return on your investment. You'll be taught what to look for when looking for a property, how to make an offer, how to identify properties with returns in excess of 25 per cent and whether or not to refurbish.

- **Find the right tenant:** Finding the right tenant is the key to the success of your investment. In chapter 4 you'll identify what tenant is best for your property, you and your lender and where to advertise. Chapter 4 will examine the benefits of credit checking, the relationships between landlord and tenant, and rent collection.

- **How to create and expand your portfolio:** How to own a multitude of properties by the secret of remortgaging and to keep your portfolio by adopting risk management techniques. Check out chapter 5.

- **Minimise tax:** Chapter 6 deals with how to avoid (but not evade!) tax in connection with property.

- **Operate legally:** Chapter 7 deals with all the legal aspects a landlord might face when investing in property. It covers the types of contracts you'll enter into, the regulations governing residential letting property and the law in general.

- **Essential references:** Chapter 8 is a one-stop shop of all the addresses, phone numbers and websites that relate to investing in property. This includes, among others, hotspot areas to invest in, lenders, insurers and accommodation projects.

CHAPTER 1

The initial investment

So to become a professional landlord you need bundles of cash – false! A portfolio can be amassed from nothing or as little as £500, as I did 11 years ago. We have access to cash reserves that we don't even know about because we're not fully aware of certain financial products on the market.

The term 'initial investment' implies that starting capital is required. However, even though it's advisable to have an initial investment, it's not mandatory in order to set up a multi-million-pound investment portfolio – no matter what business experts say. I'm sure you've heard many testimonies of multi-millionaires who started with a couple of pounds in their pocket. What made these people succeed was their attitude to risk. To become a millionaire in business you have to take a certain degree of risk. Otherwise, we would all be rich! However, I expect that many readers don't have the same attitudes to risk as the millionaires I've just mentioned. The beauty of property is that you can invest in property according to your own personal attitudes to risk.

Let's look at the risks in investing in property. There are three core elements making up the income and expenditure account – income being rent, expenditure being the mortgage payment, and maintenance. All these three elements can be fixed if need be, and as long as income exceeds expenditure, you're in the money! That's right – guaranteed profit. There are financial products out there that can guarantee rental income, fix mortgage payments and fix maintenance expenditure. Consider which risk class you fit in, based on the table below:

Risk Class	Income	Expenditure	
	Rent	**Mortgage Cost**	**Maintenance Cost**
1	Guaranteed	Nil	Fixed

If only! This is the investor who has enough cash to buy a property outright, guarantee his income, never worry about maintaining the property and still earns treble what a bank or building society will offer him.

2	Guaranteed	Fixed	Fixed

This is the investor who doesn't have bundles of cash but is willing to borrow. However, he also wants to ensure that he will meet his mortgage payment and any maintenance costs. This is someone who is risk-averse and isn't typically a handyman when it comes to household repairs.

3	Guaranteed	Fixed	Variable

This is a risk-averse investor, but he can do his own household repairs or is willing to take the risk on household repairs.

4	Guaranteed	Variable	Variable

This is an investor who accepts a fair degree of risk to interest rate fluctuations and household repairs.

5	Not Guaranteed	Fixed	Fixed

This is an investor who probably works and earns more than he spends in order to cover the mortgage and maintenance payments. Receipt of rental income is crucial, but not crucial enough to meet the fixed mortgage and maintenance payments on time. Cash flow isn't an issue for this investor in the short term.

6	Not Guaranteed	Fixed	Variable

Again, this is an investor who works and earns more than he spends. However, he is also willing to take the risk of maintaining the property because he is a handyman or is just simply willing to take the risk.

7	Not Guaranteed	Variable	Variable

The risk-taker. Here we have our future millionaire. His income is maximised because he obtains his rent in the open market, his mortgage payment is minimised because he sources the best-discounted mortgage product and he has taken full risk on maintenance hoping that nothing major will go wrong. This strategy is probably suited to investors who comfortably earn an income in excess of their spending. Cash flow is crucial.

Table 1.1 Risk classes

There are other permutations of the above model but most people fall into one of the seven categories. The higher the risk factor you are, the more money you can make, but the key factor is whichever risk factor you are, you'll make money.

The initial investment you require is completely determined by your attitude to risk. The lower your risk factor, the higher the initial investment will be. For example, an investor who falls into risk class 1 has to finance the whole purchase price of the property in order for him not to have to meet a monthly mortgage payment. Hence, he isn't dependent on the punctuality of the tenants' rent payment; this way his investment in the property market is restricted to his savings in the bank. On the other hand, someone with a risk factor 7, with nothing in the bank, can borrow on an unsecured personal loan basis. He can then use this as deposits for a number of properties on a buy-to-let mortgage scheme and acquire a number of properties.

Let's look at a specific example:

Mandy with risk class 1 and £40,000 to invest

Mandy buys a property for £40,000 in Northampton. She guarantees her rent from a rental guarantee company (see chapter 8), borrows nothing and pays for a maintenance insurance contract which covers the cost for all major incidental maintenance expenditure. Her monthly return is:

	£
Rent	450
Mortgage	0
Maintenance	25
Profit	425

Arnie with risk class 7 and £3,000 to invest

Arnie borrows £18,000 on an unsecured basis at eight per cent APR over seven years and uses this to fund three properties for £40,000 each in Northampton on a buy-to-let mortgage basis at 85 per cent 'loan to value' at six per cent APR. This means that he has to put down £6,000 each on the three properties. This adds up to £18,000 unsecured borrowings. The £3,000 that Arnie has goes towards professional fees on all three properties.

	1	2	3	Total £
Rent	500	500	500	1,500
Mortgage (interest only)	170	170	170	510
Unsecured loan (interest only)	120	120	120	360
Maintenance	0	25	50	75
Profit	210	185	160	555

Arnie earns more than Mandy but Arnie has a greater borrowing requirement. Currently this proves the principle that BORROWING IS CHEAP.

The reason for this is because the returns to be made from property are far greater than the cost of borrowing. Typically the return from property is around 20 per cent and the cost of borrowing is around six per cent at current rates. This assumes that you've chosen the right property, which this book shows you how to do in chapter 3.

Taking this example further, let's say property prices increase by ten per cent over three years. Then the total profit made by each investor by way of rental profit and capital appreciation profit over the three years is:

	Mandy (Risk Factor 1) £	Arnie (Risk Factor 7) £
Rental profit (36 months x monthly rental profit)	15,300	19,980

Capital appreciation (10% x total cost of properties bought)	4,000	12,000
Total	**19,300**	**31,980**

Comparing these two investors shows that Arnie who started with £3,000 has earned 66 per cent more than Mandy who started with £40,000! Looking at the actual return from your initial investment being:

$$\frac{\text{Profit} \times 100}{\text{Initial investment}}$$

Then the returns for each investor are as follows:

	Mandy (Risk Factor 1)	**Arnie (Risk Factor 7)**
Total profit (from the table above)	19,300	31,980
Initial investment	40,000	3,000
Return on initial investment over 3 years	48%	1,066%
Return on initial investment averaged over 1 year	16%	355%
Return on initial investment if deposited in a high interest building society account (current Bank of England base interest rate)	5%	5%

You can see that both investors have made returns in excess of any high interest building society account. You can also see that Arnie has made phenomenal returns far in excess of most investment funds or even technology stocks at their peak. The best thing is that you're investing in property, which all of us have some degree of understanding in, rather than a stock which you know little about and have to rely heavily on the financial press and tipsters.

But an even more important principle than the one above is that WHATEVER YOUR ATTITUDE TO RISK IS, YOU SHOULD MAKE MONEY!

The reality is that in the last three years we have seen average property prices grow by ten per cent every year rather than ten per cent over three years. This equates to 33 per cent capital appreciation over the three years. Thus the annual return from property over the last three years for both investors was 24 per cent and 662 per cent respectively. This example gives you an indication of how I've amassed great wealth through property, as any money invested has grown by over six times each year because I have a risk factor of 7. So every £1,000 I invested was worth £6,620 in year 1, £13,240 in year 2 and £19,860 in year 3.

In the reference chapter you'll find all the providers for guaranteed rent, buy-to-let mortgages and maintenance insurers and contractors.

Now, whatever risk factor you are, this will determine how much initial investment is needed. Assuming a property is at a purchase price of £50,000, the following initial investment will be needed:

Risk Factor	Initial Investment (£)
1	51,000
2–5	8,500 – 50,999
6	1,000
7	Nil

This assumes a 15 per cent deposit for the mortgage and £1,000 fees for solicitors, valuations and the initial void period when waiting to find the right tenant. Risk factor 6 investors borrow the initial deposit and risk factor 7 investors borrow the initial deposit and associated fees by way of secured or unsecured borrowings.

Raising the initial investment

So you've decided which risk factor you are and this has determined how much initial investment is required. How do you then go about raising the initial investment? The following table ranks, in order, the 'cost' to you, starting with the cheapest first, the cost being the effective interest rate being paid on the initial investment as a result of your choice of investing in property. BOE means current Bank of England Base Rate.

Source	Cost	Narrative
Personal assets	0%	Assets that are no longer being used but have some resale value. This may be jewellery, cars, furniture, pieces of art, electrical equipment, etc. The cost is nil as the assets are not being used, but they could be used to realise some cash in order to invest. Look in the garage or attic – you may be surprised! Think about it like this – you're trading in your Ford now for the Ferrari in five years' time!
Savings	BOE Base Rate	You may have savings in a deposit account or cash ISA. If you use this money, the cost will be the lost interest that would have been earned if you had left it in the account.
Endowment policies or company shares	BOE Base Rate +3%	You could surrender an endowment policy or liquidise a current share portfolio to raise the cash. I recommend you talk to your financial adviser and stockbroker before taking this action as you could be better off holding out on some of these policies or shares. But it could be

Source	Cost	Narrative
		time to let go of some poorly performing stocks and enter the property arena as so many of the share market investors are doing now. The cost of this on average is equivalent to the average return the stock market delivers. This, of course, will be different depending on the type of policy or stocks you hold.
Borrow from family	BOE +4%	You may have a family member who has cash sitting in the bank and is willing to lend it to you. You can offer him a better rate of return than any deposit account could. If he is a close member of the family, he may lend it to you for 0%, but if you proposition a family member offering BOE+4% you might get quite a few more positive responses than expected. You could access your inheritance early, as many families do, to avoid Inheritance Tax. As long as the giver lives seven years beyond the date of the gift, there is no Inheritance Tax to pay and this is therefore beneficial to both parties. A family member may be more willing to give you assets if you're proposing to invest them further, rather than to squander them on a new car or holiday.
Secured borrowings	BOE +2–7%	To do this, you must already own a property. The cheapest way to do this is to remortgage the

Source	Cost	Narrative
		whole property and release the equity tied up in your home. It pays to shop around. A good mortgage broker could probably beat the current rate that you're paying now and even reduce your monthly payments while still raising you some cash on top. The other way is to get a second charge loan where you keep your existing mortgage and borrow on the remaining equity on the house. You've probably seen the TV adverts promising you a new car or holiday just from one phone call. Well, forget a new car or holiday – we're going property hunting!
Unsecured borrowings	BOE +2 – 15%	The cheapest way to do this is by transferring a current credit card balance to a new credit card with introductory rate offers. You draw out as much cash as you can on your current credit card and then apply for a credit card that has a low introductory rate for balance transfers until the balance is cleared. Once your new credit card has been approved, you transfer your existing balance on your old credit card to the new credit card at the introductory rate, typically BOE+2%. This rate is fixed until you clear the balance. You may, however, not get this new credit card. The other way is to draw down the

Source	Cost	Narrative
		cash on your existing credit card at the credit card rate. This can be expensive, but if the property you've found has a high income yield, you could use the cash on a short-term basis, say one to two years, and use the profits to clear the credit card balance. You may be able to arrange an overdraft with your bank or a personal loan at around BOE+6%. You need to speak to your bank manager. You can also go to other unsecured lenders, but there are high arrangement fees and the interest rate can even go up to BOE+35%! You need to shop around, but I would advise steering clear of anything with an interest rate higher than 25% unless you're really desperate and the property you've found has a very high income yield.
Get a partner	Dependent	The other way to raise the cash is by taking on a financial partner. This means that the financial risk is borne by the partner, but you end up doing all the work. The partner will be entitled to a share of your profits and you'll not be free to do what you want with the property. Equating the cost to you will depend on how successful the property is, as the cost will be the share of profits made. Even though this is the

Source	Cost	Narrative
		most expensive way to finance a property business, it can also be the cheapest way if the whole project fails, as your partner has taken the full financial risk. If this is the only method you can use to get into property, I would still advise taking on a partner as you'll still be participating in a share of the property market.

Table 1.2 Raising the initial investment

The above table isn't an exhaustive list. You may have other good ideas for raising finance, but if you can't raise the finance, the project can't go ahead; it's as simple as that. The only other way is to change your attitude to risk. This means being willing to take a bigger risk and hence increase your risk factor, thus reducing the initial investment needed. Greater borrowings will be inevitable.

I raised my initial investment by saving as much of my salary as I could. While my colleagues were spending everything they earned on high rents on apartments, expensive holidays and designer clothes, I saved my money by living in one room in a shared house, holidaying in the UK and wearing unbranded clothes. After ten years I live in a large, 8,000ft^2 detached house, I holiday abroad at least ten times a year and wear only designer clothes. You need patience and a medium- to long-term vision if you truly desire to have enough wealth to live the lifestyle you want.

If all else fails

If you're struggling to find the initial investment there are still three further tricks you could consider:

1. Get a 100 per cent loan-to-value residential mortgage

2. Create a vendor deposit

3. Get cashback on completion

Get a 100 per cent loan to value residential mortgage

There is still one way you can acquire a property if you're a first-time buyer. There are certain lenders that provide 100 per cent residential mortgages that are free of fees. This means that the lender funds the whole purchase of the property and pays for all the valuation and solicitor's fees.

This product is for residential purposes only. However, you can make the application with the intention of living in the property, but then inform the lender when the purchase completes that you intend to let it out now as you've changed your mind. Some lenders don't mind and simply charge a letting fee of £50–£100 per year. Some lenders, usually building societies, charge additional interest, typically two per cent, on the loan. You have to look at your figures very carefully to ensure that the rent can cover the 100 per cent financing plus the additional interest if need be.

A list of 100 per cent fee-free lenders can be found in the reference chapter.

Create a vendor deposit

This is where you basically get the vendor to pay your deposit! This is best explained by following the example below:

Gavin wishes to buy an investment property for, say, £54,000, but he only has £3,000 to invest. The minimum deposit he needs is 15 per cent of £54,000, which equals £8,100. You may think he cannot go ahead as he has a shortfall of £5,100.

However, if he gets the vendor to inflate the purchase price to £60,000, then the deposit required is 15 per cent of £60,000, which equals £9,000. If he also gets the vendor to contribute £6,000 and Gavin contributes £3,000, with the total contribution being £9,000, then Gavin can purchase the property.

This can best be shown by the following table:

	Without Vendor Deposit £	With Vendor Deposit £
Purchase price	54,000	60,000

Deposit required (assume 15% of purchase price)	8,100	9,000
Gavin's actual investment	3,000	3,000
Shortfall of investment = Deposit required minus Gavin's actual investment	5,100	6,000
Vendor contribution = Inflated purchase price minus purchase price	N/A	6,000
Actual shortfall = Shortfall of investment minus vendor contribution	5,100	Nil

Here, the vendor gets:

£60,000 minus £6,000 = £54,000

The inflated price minus vendor contribution = original asking price

Gavin gets an investment property costing £54,000 for a £3,000 initial investment and he manages to increase the amount he can borrow from the mortgage lender. His borrowings are now greater than 85 per cent loan to value as he now has borrowed 85 per cent of £60,000. Everybody's a winner.

This trick is completely legal, but relies on the property being valued at a higher figure. This is likely because of three reasons:

- **Valuers don't like to down-value a property**, unless there is something wrong with it! If they think the purchase price is only slightly higher than what it's worth, they will always value it at the purchase price. This is because the valuer knows that valuations are not an exact science. Valuations are based on what people will pay for a property and he will assume that if you're willing to pay, say,

£60,000, then the property is probably worth £60,000. A ten per cent gross inflation of the purchase price isn't a lot considering you're only talking about an inflation of £6,000. For higher value properties (greater than £200,000) I would suggest a five per cent vendor deposit contribution as a £10,000 purchase price inflation could be contested.

- **You may be getting a bargain property**, i.e. the property is worth £60,000 but you're actually getting it for £54,000, hence it values up to £60,000.

- **Valuers are under pressure to value properties at the purchase price.** Lenders make money by lending money. If they instruct a firm of valuers that keep on down-valuing properties, then it becomes difficult for the lender to lend and hence make money. The more the valuer values property at the purchase price, the more money the lender makes. Especially in the current rising property price conditions, even if the valuer thinks that the purchase price is one per cent or two per cent inflated, he will assume that it will reach the valuation in a few months anyway.

There are tax issues. The vendor has to declare the inflated sales price to HM Revenue & Customs and, at the time of writing, he will therefore have to pay more Capital Gains Tax as his gain is deemed to be higher. For the vendor this may not be a problem as the HM Revenue & Customs gives you an allowance in excess of £7,000 for a capital gain. If this inflated price doesn't take the gain above this allowance, then there is no increased Capital Gains Tax to pay. (For the latest information on Capital Gains Tax allowances, please refer to HM Revenue & Customs' website at www.hmrc.gov.uk.)

Get cashback on completion

This is similar to creating a vendor deposit as it requires the property to be valued higher than the agreed price. You see cashback on completion offered by some car dealers on new cars when you take out finance on a new car. It's effectively a discount on the sales price.

Cashback on completion means exactly what it says. You receive cashback when you complete the transaction.

Let me use the same example as the one in 'Create a vendor deposit' to explain this. Assume that Gavin wants to buy a property at £54,000 and he only has £3,000 to invest. Let's assume the vendor agrees to sell the property at £60,000 with £6,000 cashback:

	Without Cashback £	With Cashback £
Purchase price	54,000	60,000
Deposit required (assume 15% of purchase price)	(8,100)	(9,000)
Deposit paid on exchange of contracts (assume 5%)	2,700	3,000
Deposit required to complete (remaining 10%)	5,400	6,000
Amount left to invest = £3,000 minus deposit paid on exchange	300	Nil
Shortfall = Deposit required to complete minus amount left to invest	5,100	6,000
Cashback	nil	6,000
Actual shortfall = Shortfall minus cashback	5,100	Nil

Here, the vendor gets his asking price of £54,000 which is the inflated price minus the cashback:

£60,000 minus £6,000 = £54,000

and Gavin gets an investment property costing £54,000 with £3,000 initial investment.

The same rules apply to upward valuation and Capital Gains Tax mentioned above.

CHAPTER 2

Finding the right buy-to-let mortgage provider

If you're funding the whole purchase of the property yourself, then you can skip this chapter, as it deals with obtaining further borrowings to finance the property purchase.

A buy-to-let mortgage is a relatively new financial product, emerging onto the market in 1995, which allows anybody to purchase a house or flat with the intention of letting it out. This product allows you to borrow the finance needed to buy a property based on the rental income generated rather than on your actual personal income. Typically, as long as the rental income is greater than 130 per cent of the interest payment, you could purchase the property, but this, of course, can vary depending on your mortgage.

For a buy-to-let mortgage, you typically need 15–25 per cent of the purchase price as a deposit, so for a £40,000 purchase price you would need between £6,000 and £10,000 and the lender would fund the other £30,000 to £34,000. A higher deposit is needed in comparison to a residential property, where the deposit needed is typically 0–10 per cent, as with a buy-to-let mortgage the property isn't owner-occupied and the lender's mortgage payment depends on a suitable and reliable tenant being found. Hence, this presents a higher risk to the lender. If it ever has to repossess the property, it would only need to achieve 85 per cent of the purchase price. This may only be the true market value of the property after it has been tenanted or if there is a property slump at the time of repossession.

There are a few 90 per cent LTV lenders out there (only a few!), which means that you only have to put down a ten per cent deposit. To find out these 90 per cent lenders, please see chapter 8, the reference chapter.

What's best for you?

The most suitable buy-to-let mortgage for you depends on the following factors:

1. Your initial investment

2. The purchase price

3. The type of property

4. Your personal credit history

5. Your attitude to risk

6. The degree of aftercare

7. Duration of borrowing and maximising cash flow

Your initial investment

The initial investment dictates the maximum purchase price. This is best explained in an example:

Investor A has £7,000 to invest. He assumes £1,000 for professional fees and the initial void period, leaving a £6,000 deposit. Considering that the maximum loan to value (LTV) is 85 per cent, the greatest purchase price is:

£6,000/0.15 = £40,000

The maximum he can borrow is therefore £34,000. So the following formula holds:

$$\frac{\text{(Initial investment minus professional fees)} = }{\text{Deposit required/100}} \text{maximum purchase price}$$

It's crucial to calculate the maximum purchase price so you know what you can afford to buy. It's also important to ensure that your maximum purchase price is in excess of the lender's minimum purchase price – see below.

The purchase price

Almost all lenders have a minimum purchase price. The minimum purchase price starts at £6,500 and rises up to £75,000 for certain lenders. If your purchase price is below the lender's minimum purchase price, then the lender will not consider you under any circumstances. So the purchase price can dictate the mortgage you can get.

The type of property

Lenders have certain exclusions based on the type of property it is. The key exclusions are:

1. **Studio flats:** These are flats that have one main room that is used as a lounge and bedroom, plus a kitchen and a bathroom. They are excluded, as they can be difficult to sell if there was a property price slump.

2. **Ex-local authority houses and flats:** These are properties that were once owned by the local council and subsequently sold on to private people. They are excluded, as they are associated with the lower end of the property market.

3. **Flats above commercial properties:** These are excluded as the commercial property below could be let out to an Indian or Chinese take-away at some later date. Because of the smell of the food it would lead to a decline in the market value of the property.

4. **Flats with more than four storeys:** These will be considered a high-rise block and at the lower end of the property market.

5. **Multiple-title properties:** These are properties where a freehold exists with a number of long leases and you're trying to buy the freehold. An example of this is a block of flats.

6. **Non-standard construction:** If a house isn't built of brick or doesn't have a pitched tile roof, it's deemed non-standard. For example, some houses may be constructed from poured concrete. Despite being perfectly fine houses, lenders may consider these properties inferior to standard construction properties.

The type of property can dictate the mortgage you can get.

Your personal credit history

What the lender is trying to establish is: are you a good bet? It needs to know that it will get its money back plus interest, with the minimum of effort. It needs to establish whether you're creditworthy.

There are two main credit reference agencies that all lenders consult before they make any lending decision: Experian and Equifax. They record a number of details about you based on your current and previous addresses in the last three years, namely:

1. **Electoral Roll:** Details of whether you're on the Electoral Roll; some lenders require you to be on it before they can lend.

2. **County Court Judgments (CCJs):** These arise when a debtor has taken you to court to enforce payment of a debt and the debtor won the case. The court holds this information for six years from the date of the judgment. They also record if you subsequently paid the judgment.

3. **Individual Voluntary Arrangements (IVAs):** This is where you've become bankrupt and unable to pay your debts. Once you've been made bankrupt and the debts have been settled, then you become a discharged bankrupt. Only once you've been discharged can you have any hope of obtaining credit again. You're automatically discharged after six years.

4. **Credit accounts:** These are all your loan accounts that have been active in the last six years and whether you've ever defaulted on them. Typical accounts are your mortgage account, credit and store card accounts and personal loans.

5. **Repossessions:** Details of any repossessions of your homes that have ever occurred.

6. **Previous searches:** These are previous credit searches by other lenders that you've made a credit application with.

7. **Gone Away Information Network (GAIN):** This is where you've moved home and not forwarded on the new address and not satisfied the debt.

8. **Credit Industry Fraud Avoidance System (CIFAS):** This is where the lender suspects fraud and just flags it up; you cannot be refused credit based on a suspicion.

Your credit file dictates the mortgage you can get. The key factors are CCJs or defaults. If you have any CCJs or defaults (points 2 and 4 above), you'll be restricted to adverse credit lenders that charge higher arrangement fees and interest rates. If you have an IVA, repossession or GAIN on your file, it's unlikely that you'll get a buy-to-let mortgage, but you'll still probably be able to get a residential mortgage depending on when you had debt problems. It's worth noting that the buy-to-let mortgage market is always developing and a suitable product may come on to the market soon.

There is one key thing you should remember when filling out your form – don't lie! If your lender finds out, it will demand repayment in full and it could inform the police of fraud – the charge being obtaining finance by deception. The credit reference agencies are becoming more and more sophisticated. They log every bit of information you put on every credit application and if you submit an application that was slightly different from a previous application, they will flag it up.

Your attitude to risk

As discussed earlier, your attitude to risk is key to the level of exposure you want to have over events that are out of your control. When it comes to mortgages, the only real risk is the interest rate. There are only two categories of type of interest rate – fixed or variable. There are various sub-categories of this in the table below:

	Type	Narrative
Fixed	Fixed	This is for the low risk-taker. It ensures that the monthly mortgage payment is fixed for a period of time, usually between one and ten years.
	Capped	This is also for a low risk-taker. It ensures that the mortgage payment never exceeds a certain amount but if interest rates fall, then your mortgage payment can fall. No downside risk and only upside potential!
Variable	Tracker	This is where the interest rate being charged follows the exact rate being set by the Bank of England plus a buy-to-let interest loading, typically 1–2%. You're fully exposed to the Bank of England interest rate fluctuations.
	Discount	This is where the initial interest rate is discounted by 1–4% for a specified period of time. This could be a discount on a tracker or a standard variable rate. You're exposed but, because there is a discount in place, you don't feel the fluctuations quite as badly.
	Stepped	This is where the discount is reduced over a number of years. So you would be entitled to a 3% discount in year 1, 2% discount in year 2 and 1% discount in year 3, for example.

Type	Narrative
Variable	This is just the standard variable rate set by the lender. Your mortgage payments are fully exposed to interest rate fluctuations.

Table 2.1 Types of interest rate

You have to be careful of the tie-in/lock-in periods that may exist with all these products. These are the minimum periods that you have to remain with the lender without incurring financial penalties if you wish to redeem the loan because you want to sell or remortgage the property.

Some lenders provide all the mortgages above and some lenders only provide some of these mortgages. The type of mortgage you want dictates the lender you have to approach.

The degree of aftercare

Some people require face-to-face contact with their lender. If this is so, then you can really only approach high street banks and building societies. There are many lenders who don't talk to the public and who will only liaise with a mortgage broker. Personally, I don't mind not having face-to-face contact, as my mortgage broker is quite efficient in handling my queries.

Duration of borrowing and maximising cash flow

The duration of the loan needs to meet your own personal criteria. This depends on your age, personal goals and cash flow. You may wish to own the property outright by a certain age. This means that you require a mortgage that is less than the normal 25-year period or a flexible mortgage where the interest is charged daily and can be settled whenever you want.

You may require an interest only mortgage rather than a repayment mortgage, so that your monthly payments are lower. This will maximise your cash flow. Not all lenders provide flexible or interest only mortgages, so if this is what you require it will limit your choice.

Typical profile

So after considering the seven factors dictating the type of mortgage you can get, you can build a profile that looks like this:

Factor	Profile
Maximum purchase price	£50,000
The purchase price	£45,000
The type of property	Private one-bedroom flat standard construction

Factor	Profile
Your personal credit history	Clean
Fixed or variable?	Fixed capped (no lock-in period)
The degree of aftercare	High street bank or building society
Duration of borrowing and maximising cash flow	25 years and interest only

With this profile you can approach a mortgage broker and he will be able to source a lender that meets your profile. I would advise that you make an application with a lender before you find the property, so that when you do find a property you can act quickly if need be.

CHAPTER 3

Finding the right property

So you've got the finance in place, now you need to find the property. This is the most important decision in the whole process. It's the property you choose that dictates your success. There are many properties on the market but less than one per cent are worth buying.

During the whole property investment process there is only one figure you can ever be in control of: the purchase price. If the price is too high, then you can walk away. You only ever become involved in the whole property purchase process when the price is right. But what is the right price?

There is a rule of thumb that I always apply when looking for a property to invest in – I call it 'the rule of 12'. It's very simple to remember when looking at properties.

Let's assume the purchase price is £45,000. Knock off the two zeros at the end (in effect, divide the purchase price by 100) and you arrive at £450. This then determines the monthly rental figure that needs to be charged to obtain a 12 per cent gross yield. Gross yield is defined as:

$$\frac{\text{Annual rental income} \times 100}{\text{Property purchase price}} = \text{gross yield}$$

If you can achieve a 12 per cent yield, then go for it! Speak to letting agents or look in the local press for typical rental values for the area that you're looking at. This yield is also stated as a payback period – the length of time it would take to own the property if you reinvested all the income earned to replenish your savings. You would calculate it as follows:

$$\frac{1}{\text{Gross yield}/100} \qquad = \qquad \text{payback period}$$

So in this example the payback period would be 8.33 years.

12 per cent is a like-for-like comparison to a bank or building society rate. So if your bank is offering four per cent, you know that you can earn three times as much from investing in property. But this assumes that you've funded the whole property purchase out of your own funds. Usually this isn't the case. When you borrow to finance the purchase, the returns are significantly higher as highlighted in chapter 1.

When you become familiar with an area and its rental values, then you know when a property is a bargain. If typical rental values for a one-bedroom flat are £500 per month, then you instantly know if you walk past an agent's window and there's a flat advertised for £46,000, that you're going to get in excess of 12 per cent so it's worth an enquiry.

If, however, flats in the area are rarely priced under £70,000, then forget that area! You're not going to make any money there. It's the price that will dictate the area. Forget location, location, location; it's PRICE, PRICE, PRICE! This is because you're looking for a property to invest in rather than to live in.

It's surprisingly easy to manage a property outside your area once the property is set up right. There are many areas that offer you a return of 12 per cent and greater. Areas like these I call hotspots. In the reference chapter is a list of all the hotspots I've identified with their gross yields of 12 per cent and greater.

What if you cannot find a 12 per cent yield?

I know it can be frustrating trying to find a property that meets the rule of 12. I know this because I feel this frustration on a weekly basis! But to make money on property you have to stick to certain rules and if you're going to stick to only one rule, make sure that it's the rule of 12.

The reason for this is because the rule of 12 is the foundation of property investment success for 'poor people'.

If you're trying to build a property portfolio out of very little (like I did with only £500), you need a healthy rental income to pay for all the borrowings you take on. If you borrow at a six per cent interest rate, then there is no point buying a property that yields at six per cent AT BEST (being 100 per cent occupancy and zero repair costs for the year) as you'll only break even. If you're banking on capital growth, then you're simply banking on speculation. I never believe in speculation as the future is completely unknown.

What about capital appreciation?

Capital appreciation is the amount the property rises in value over time. I never include the gains by capital appreciation in my calculation of yields because it's an unknown figure at the point you make the investment. If there was any certainty of the capital appreciation of a property, then the purchase price of the property would include this gain. As there is a lot of uncertainty over capital appreciation because of the numerous variables involved, it's very difficult to predict when house prices will rise. Remember, the gain is only realised when you sell the property and the difficult thing with any investment is knowing when to get out and sell.

I see capital appreciation as a bonus. I focus on the investment as it stands. If it makes money now, it will almost certainly make you money in the future. If the property prices crash, who cares! You're still making money as the rent rises with inflation and the mortgage payment is still the same. If property prices soar, great! You can realise that equity by remortgaging or by selling and buying further properties! This way there is no downside risk and only upside potential.

Admittedly, there is a lot of money to be made in capital appreciation speculation, but this should be left to the professional property investors. They have the time to research the market and they can stomach the loss if there is a property price crash.

What to do in the event of a crash

There are only two words to what you should do in the event of a crash: NEVER SELL!

This is such a key point. A loss is only ever realised once you sell. Crashes come and go, so just because your investment property's value has halved – what real difference does this make to you? The tenant is still there, the rent has remained the same and you still own the property.

I'm of the opinion that if there is a property price crash, you should buy more! If you still have a good credit line and you're in the property game for the long term, then I'm sure that property prices will bounce back (as they always do!) and you can say hello to property billionairedom, rather than millionairedom!

How to achieve a higher return of 12 per cent

I have a property in Harlow, Essex that is a five-bedroom, two-bathroom property. I used to let it out to a large family – husband, wife and seven children! I was achieving around 12 per cent return and I was quite happy. I thought they would stay there for a long time, as there is a real shortage of five-bedroomed properties to rent, let alone buy. However, in business nothing is guaranteed and they decided to move out. So I readvertised the property and an 'accommodation project' approached me.

An accommodation project is a non-profit organisation, usually a charity or local government-funded body, that assists the homeless in the town or city in which they're based. The project suggested to me that it would like to convert the property into five single units for people on housing benefit and it would handle the management for no charge. The conversion costs were minimal, simply installing independent locks on the door, providing cheap single beds in each room and basic kitchen appliances.

The project said I would be able to charge on average £70 per week for each room, which equated to £1,515 per calendar month. I compared this to what I was originally getting of £600 per month and thought I should give it a go. I had to pay all the utility bills and Council Tax, but even after that my net profit was set to increase fivefold. I've been running this scheme for five years now and I've never looked back. I even converted another one of my two-bedroom properties into a three-bedroomed place (converting the living room into another bedroom) to cash in on such a scheme.

It hasn't been without problems, though. The five-bedroom place is let to five guys of all ages and they can be quite boisterous. I've had complaints from the neighbours and environmental health, but they haven't closed me down yet. The property requires more time and effort, but that is expected considering the high yield that one is obtaining.

If you consider this type of property, go for a property that can have four lettable rooms. This could be a four-bedroom property, or a three-bedroom two-reception property (converting one reception room into another bedroom), and see if you can get two bathrooms (even if one of the bathrooms is a shower room). I would set the yield required at 33 per cent. This means that you would need £20,000 rental income for a purchase price of £60,000. For example, if the property had five rooms, then you would require an average room rate of £77 per room (£20,000/52 weeks/five rooms).

Expect to visit this property every fortnight to make sure nothing has been damaged or there are no other people staying round other than the tenants. Also, remember that, legally, letting a property as individual rooms binds you to the Houses in Multiple Occupation Bill, which includes legal and management requirements regarding a licensing scheme and energy efficiency. See chapter 7 on legal aspects regarding the rules on letting properties as a house in multiple occupation (HMO).

A list of accommodation projects can be found in the reference chapter. I would suggest you speak to them before entering into a venture, as they will be able to assess the likely demand and typical room rates.

Refurbishment

Should you refurbish a property? If you're new to the property game, I would advise you not to. It's time-consuming, you can easily be conned by builders, it's stressful and you lose money while the property is unlet. When viewing a prospective property, if it has had the kitchen or bathroom ripped out, forget it. By the time you've refurbished it you would have spent at least £5,000 in repair costs and interest and you would have built up an affection for the property. It will take you a long time to recoup the money and because you've invested a lot of your time on the property, you may be too choosy over the right tenant to move in. I mean, do you really want to be sacrificing your evenings and weekends refurbishing a wreck? No! You want to be on the high street spending all that money you're earning from making the right property investments.

If you're a bit experienced and you have the time and can afford the initial negative cash flow, then a good return can be had if the property is very cheap. As a rule of thumb, I'm interested in properties such as these if they can provide a return of 24 per cent or greater. Here you're paying less than £20,000 for a rental value of £400 per month. Always remember to double all initial budgeted refurbishment costs as experience shows that unforeseen problems emerge.

What to look for when viewing a property

Don't believe the myth that a property is only worth buying if you could see yourself living there. The fact is that you're not going to live there, so what is the point of asking yourself if you could? You should ask, 'Would someone live here?' In a high-demand area people will live in a house as long as it has running hot water. I'm sure you've heard the horror stories from people living in London. I knew of 16 Australian and New Zealand backpackers sharing one room! I wouldn't live there, but the landlord found 16 people who would! You have to assess the demand.

The best way to assess the demand is to put a rogue advert in the local press. Place an advert before you own any property in that area for a property at market value rent. See how many calls you get. If you get one or two calls, then forget it. However, if you get more than 40 calls ,then you know you've hit a hotspot. I have a few properties in Harlow, Essex and I placed an advert for one of my properties at slightly above market value and I had at least 40 calls and the property was let within two hours of the paper coming out.

When viewing a property check the following:

Kitchen	Is the kitchen big enough to accommodate a small dining table? This is attractive if there is only one reception room and it turns the kitchen into a kitchen-diner.
Smallest bedroom	If the smallest bedroom is smaller than 6' 6" in any direction, then it's not a bedroom! You

	need to be able to get a bed in a bedroom, hence this room can only be considered as a study or a baby's room. You need to consider this when considering what type of tenant you're looking for. If you're looking for two professional people to share a two-bedroom flat, then the second bedroom must be bigger than 6' 6".
Bathroom	Is there a fitted shower? A bathroom is a lot more desirable if there is a power shower. If there are two bathrooms, then the property is very desirable, even if it's only a shower room.
Heating	Is the heating system old? This can be costly to replace. If possible, get it checked prior to purchase. It's your legal duty to provide heating and to issue a gas safety record.
Electrics	Are the electric sockets old? This will tell you that at some point the whole electric system will need rewiring.
Service charges	If it's a flat, you'll have to pay service charges. Ask the agent if he has any details of the service charges. Some places have exorbitant service charges that render the whole investment unprofitable. Avoid listed buildings as they have frequent redecoration policies that can be expensive.

If the property is in a reasonable condition, then buy it. If demand is good, there should be no problem letting it out as long as the property is in reasonable condition.

Making an offer

If you suspect that there will be a lot of interest in the property because it's cheap, don't be afraid simply to offer the asking price. This way there is no to-ing and fro-ing, the deal is done on the day and the property is removed from the market. If the agent gets the asking price, there is no need for him to show the property to someone else.

If you've arranged your mortgage, give a copy of the acceptance letter from the lender to the estate agent. This will convince him that you can act quickly, you're serious about buying the property and you're not just someone off the street who thinks he can make some money out of it without giving it much thought. If you can show the agent your bank statement as well, which proves that you have the deposit, then do so. Anything that will convince the agent that you're serious will make him unlikely to show the property to someone else.

If you suspect that demand isn't high for the property, but it's still a sound investment, then ask the agent how long it has been on the market. If it's been a while, then make a low offer. I would say 75–80 per cent of the asking price. Ask the estate agent, 'Has it ever had an offer? What offers have been refused?' Then you'll be able to gauge your entry offer. This is assuming that you believe the agent! If you've built up a relationship with an agent, this shouldn't be an issue, but always be aware.

Always remember the rule of 12 when negotiating. Don't get carried away with the negotiations and put in an offer that breaks the rule of 12.

When the offer is accepted, the agent will almost certainly ask you for your solicitor's details. Have your solicitor arranged prior to placing an offer. Simply inform a solicitor that you'll be using him for a future purchase. The agent will then write to your solicitor to confirm the sale and the solicitor will instruct you what to do from then on.

You have to be patient when buying properties. Under normal circumstances the purchase should take no longer than eight weeks from the date your offer was accepted. There are many things that can go wrong with a purchase and sometimes there is nothing you can do about it but sit back and wait. Here is a list of some of the things that can go wrong and what, if possible, you can do about them:

What can go wrong	What to do about it
The vendor withdraws the property from the market.	If the vendor has decided to keep the property, there is nothing you can do about it. If he has decided to sell to someone else, then find out the selling

What can go wrong	What to do about it
	price and go in even higher. If the property is worth more, then pay it! Remember, don't forget the rule of 12.
The survey fails or the surveyor undervalues the property.	Find out what the property failed on. Ask the vendor to remedy the problems. Don't, under any circumstances, offer to contribute to the cost of any remedial work. This is because if he then remedies the problems, he may not sell the property to you and you'll find it difficult to get your money back. If the property has been undervalued, it's difficult to persuade the valuer to value it up, but it's worth a try. Consider approaching another lender for a revaluation or think about contributing the difference between the purchase price and the valuation.
The mortgage company requires documentation at the last minute, but you don't have the documentation or it it will take a long time to get it.	Kick up a fuss! If the lender has approved your mortgage but it then wants further documentation, it should have asked for it earlier. Threaten to complain to the Financial Services Authority (FSA). If all else fails, try to get a compromise, i.e. if it wants your mortgage statement to prove that you've kept up to date on your mortgage payments in the last 12 months, offer the lender your bank statements for the last 12 months.
The flow of documentation between solicitors is slow or non-existent.	Ring your estate agent and get him to chase for you. The agent's wages depend on the sale of the property so he will have an interest in the sale occurring sooner rather than later. Ring your solicitor and ask what the hold-up is. Ask your solicitor if there is anything you can

What can go wrong	What to do about it
	do. If you really want the property, you have to be prepared to do some of the acquisition work yourself. If it's proving impossible to get certain documentation from the freeholders when buying the leasehold, then consider losing the property. This is because when it comes to selling the property you'll probably have the same problems and purchasers will get fed up and pull out.

If things are progressing normally, however, then let your solicitor do everything, as this is what you're paying him for. Only react when your solicitor has informed you of a problem or you haven't heard anything for six weeks.

It's advisable, prior to exchange of contracts, that you view the property to see that it's still in the state you first viewed it, as exchanged contracts are legally binding. If kitchen appliances were included in the sale, then check that they remain there. Check that the carpets and curtains remain and that the condition of the property hasn't deteriorated.

Once the purchase is complete, you then have the task of finding the right tenant...

Buying at auction

I've never bought a property at auction. The main reason being that you have to be able to proceed quickly. This means that the property has to be paid in full within 21–28 days, otherwise you lose your deposit, which could be as much as 25 per cent of the purchase price. If you're getting a mortgage on the property, then the lender has to be able to act quickly as well. Unfortunately, I don't have much faith in lenders to act quickly enough to ensure that payment is received in time.

There are definitely bargains to be had. If you have the nerves to buy at auction, then I recommend you follow these ten steps created by Giulia De Marco from Gold solicitors:

Step 1 – Go to an auction!

Most property auctions are open to the public. If you're interested, the best preparation starts with going along and getting a feel for what happens. It will also help to get rid of any unfounded fears; for example, you'll not end up having to buy a property just because you nodded your head at the wrong time!

Step 2 – Register

Register with all the known auctioneers in the UK. They will put you on their mailing list and send you their auction catalogues. Catalogues usually give you a guide price for each property. It's important to note that this isn't a valuation of the property; it's only an estimate of what the auctioneers or their clients expect the property to fetch at auction. There is no guarantee that the property will fetch that price and often it can go for considerably more than the guide price (and, it can go for less). Also, it shouldn't be considered as a basis for the valuation which a surveyor might give the property.

Step 3 – Get the sales schedule and view

Once you have your catalogue, you may see some properties of interest. Telephone the auctioneers and see if they have any more details on the property or a sales schedule. They will also tell you the arrangements for viewing the property.

Step 4 – Instruct your solicitor

If you have viewed the property and wish to proceed, it's very important that you contact your solicitor as soon as possible. The sooner you instruct your solicitor, the sooner he can advise you on all matters. If you instruct your solicitor on the day of the auction or after successfully bidding, the solicitor is limited on what advice and action he can give you. Leave plenty of time for your solicitor to be able to provide you with the fullest assistance and advice.

The purchase of a property at an auction is entirely different from purchasing a property being privately marketed. For example, if you're successful in your bid at the auction, you're immediately committed to proceeding or you face the possibility of being sued for breach of contract. Another example is that the contract to purchase the property at auction may specify that you take the title as it exists. This and the other conditions that apply depend on what the legal package is for that particular property. Your solicitor would wish, therefore, to examine the title deeds and legal package and provide you with a full report prior to you bidding at the auction. You or your solicitor may also wish to make enquiries of the local authority and carry out other searches all before the date of the auction. The moral of this is that the early bird catches the worm (and all the best bird houses!).

Step 5 – Financing

If you're going to bid for a property at an auction, then you'll be committing yourself on the day. It's therefore important to ensure that you have all the necessary financing of this transaction in place.

If you're seeking to obtain a mortgage over the property, then the lender will require a survey of the property to be carried out. Even if you're purchasing the property by cash, it's still recommended that you carry out a survey. It's important to know exactly what you're purchasing! What seemed a very competitive price at auction might not be if you discover that you have to spend £10,000 on remedying timber defects which you had not budgeted for. If you're obtaining a mortgage, it's even more important that you contact your solicitor in good time. Your mortgage offer will have conditions attached and it's important that your solicitor can check that these conditions can be complied with. Remember, your solicitor will be able to assist in appointing a surveyor or interpreting the survey results.

Step 6 – Bidding

If, after consultation with your solicitor and surveyor, you decide to bid at the auction, there are a couple of important things to note.

Don't worry, swatting at that fly or developing a nervous tic will not result with you being the proud owner of a holiday cottage in Shetland when you were looking for a townhouse in Glasgow!

If you're successful on the day of auction, then you'll have to pay a deposit; this must be arranged prior to the auction. It's usually around ten per cent, but it can vary. It has to be in cleared funds that are cash or a banker's draft. The auctioneer will advise what is acceptable.

If you're unable to attend the auction in person, it may be possible to bid by proxy or by telephone, but you must contact the auctioneers beforehand to arrange this.

It's important that you check on the day of the auction whether there have been any amendments which have been made that would have an effect on the title of the property or the value of the property. If you're uncertain about the effect of any alterations, then contact your solicitor or surveyor for advice. Also check that the property hasn't been withdrawn from the auction or sold prior to the auction. Sometimes the seller will consider a pre-auction offer and it may be worthwhile investigating this option.

When you're bidding for the property, ensure that you don't get carried away by offering more than you can afford. Do your budgeting beforehand and stick to it. Remember, once you've signed up on the day, you've entered into a contract. After you've completed your bid, you'll be approached by one of the auctioneer's clerks and you'll be asked to provide your details. This will include your name, address, telephone number, method of payment of the deposit and some proof of identification. A contract will then be prepared for your signature.

Step 7 – Successful bid

If your bid is successful, this isn't the end; rather, it's just the beginning. For instance, it may be a condition that you're required to insure the property straight away. Your solicitor will explain these and other conditions. The date of entry will normally be 28 days later, when the remainder of the purchase price is paid. This again will be stipulated in the contract.

Step 8 – Unsuccessful bid

If a property doesn't reach the reserve price at the auction, then the auctioneers may withdraw it. It's always worth leaving your details with the auctioneers afterwards as the seller may consider a lower price shortly after the auction.

Step 9 – From contract to settlement

Again, as soon as you've been successful, contact your solicitor, who will complete the conveyancing. This will include that in exchange for payment of the full price you'll obtain a title to the property. This title is a deed, which is registered in the Public Registers and is of importance in establishing all your rights to the property.

Step 10 – Doubts

If you're still in any doubts, contact your solicitor. Best of luck!

A list of all auction houses can be found in the reference chapter.

Buying property at auction is covered in more depth in Lawpack's book *Buying Bargains at Property Auctions* by Howard Gooddie.

CHAPTER 4

Finding the right tenant

It's no good just finding a tenant. It has to be the right tenant. What defines the right tenant will depend on the following factors:

1. The property
2. You!
3. Your lender

The property

If you've acquired a private one-bedroom riverside apartment in a central location, then a single mum on benefits is probably not the most suitable tenant. When looking at properties, it's a good idea to build up a picture of the tenant you think is most suited to it. A tenant can only fall into one of eight general categories based on the size of the family unit and whether he is working or claiming benefit. The table on pages 40–1 suggests which property is suited to each category of tenant.

So, if you buy a private one-bedroom flat, you know that the right tenant is a working single person or couple. You need only advertise for that tenant – 'suit working person or couple', the advert might read. If you misplace a tenant at your property, it will only lead to the hassle of finding another tenant later on. It's worth noting that a two+-bedroom ex-local authority house meets six out of the eight tenant categories.

You could use this table to dictate the type of property you buy. For example, if there are a lot of single parent DSS claimants in the area looking for properties, then a two-bedroom ex-local authority flat might be the right property to go for. If you wish to go for the minimum risk route, then go for the two+-bedroom ex-local authority house.

You!

If you're going to manage the property yourself, then the most important person in this whole tenant-choosing process is YOU! If you feel you can get on and deal with only a certain category of people, then choose them exclusively. If you're a professional person used to dealing with only professional people, then steer towards private properties in the nicer areas and vice versa.

Personally, I have no prejudices or hang ups – apart from two:

1. People who can't speak English
2. Young couples under 25

It can be very difficult to extract rent from tenants when you cannot communicate with them. If there is an initial language barrier, then I can foresee only problems. Unless there is an intermediary, such as a social services officer because social services are paying the rent, then it's OK. Otherwise, I would steer clear of such tenants.

	Claiming benefit	Working
Single person	Ex-local authority studio or one-bedroom flat. If you're running a rent-a-room scheme, then a room in an ex-local authority house.	Any – he may require just a room to lay his head or require a three-bedroom house because he wants a computer room and a spare room. If he can pay the rent, then he can dictate where he wants to live.
Single parent	Two-bedroom + ex-local authority	Two-bedroom ex-local authority or private house

	Claiming benefit	Working
	flat. If you let a one-bedroom flat to him, he will only be looking to move to somewhere bigger and you'll have to find another tenant again.	is preferable, as it will have a garden.
Couple	Ex-local authority studio/one-bedroom flat only. DSS are unlikely to pay market rent for a two-bedroom flat for a couple when they can quite comfortably live in a studio/one-bedroom flat.	Any – for the same reasons as above.
Family	Two+-bedroom ex-local authority house. A family will invariably want a property with a garden.	Two+-bedroom ex-local authority or private house. A family will invariably want a property with a garden.

Table 4.1 The eight categories of tenant

Couples aged under 25 are always troublesome. The tenancy will only last as long as the relationship does. They think it's a great idea to move in together after knowing each other for only two months, but when the couple fall out, neither one takes responsibility for the rent. You're left with the task of chasing them both independently for the rent, but when they blame each other, and you're the loser. If a couple under 25 are the only ones interested in the property, ask them how long they have been together and if they have lived together before. Try to get a larger deposit – two months is ideal.

Your lender

If you're borrowing to finance the property purchase, then lenders often stipulate what type of tenant you can have. The main exclusions are DSS claimants and student lets. You need to check with the lenders what exclusions they have and let this be the criteria for your selection of the lender.

Advertising for a tenant

There are six main ways of advertising for a tenant, the cheapest form of advertising first:

1. Contacting the local council (FREE)
2. Advertising with large local employers (FREE)
3. Contacting accommodation projects (FREE)
4. On the internet (possibly free)
5. Advertising in the local press
6. Through a letting agent

Contacting the local council

Councils have a waiting list of people looking for a place to live. Since councils have fewer council properties on their books, they are always pleased to hear from private landlords willing to let their properties to residents in the local area. The councils have lists of working and unemployed people, as well as refugees and asylum seekers.

I would advise that you write a letter detailing the property you have to let to the housing section of the local council and follow it up with a phone call. Councils can be slow, so I wouldn't rely on this as your only source of finding a tenant.

Advertising with large local employers

There are two large local employers in the Harlow area. I wrote to both of their human resources departments detailing that I had various properties for their employees. I get a call once every other month, so I wouldn't rely on this as your only source of finding a tenant.

Contacting local accommodation projects

Local accommodation projects are always on the lookout for willing landlords to take on homeless people in the area. Homeless doesn't mean that they are currently living rough – they simply don't have a fixed place of accommodation. These projects usually collect the rent and guarantee the rent if the tenant fails to pay. They don't charge for their services, as they are charities or non-profit organisations.

A list of accommodation projects is included in the reference chapter at the back.

On the internet

There are numerous sites on the web for landlords and tenants alike. Examples of sites where you can place an advertisement for free are:

www.letsdirect.co.uk
www.loot.com
www.roomsforlet.co.uk

Advertising in the local press

This is probably the most effective way of advertising. It's best to advertise in a paper that is delivered free locally so that your advert reaches every resident in that area. There are certain key elements you need to put in your advert:

- **Area:** You must say where the property is. It's no good to assume that the reader will know the area where the property is when the newspaper is distributed in a number of local areas. This way you avoid unwanted calls.

- **Private:** If it's in a private area (i.e. not ex-local authority), that is a selling point.

- **Furnished:** Again, if it's furnished, say so.

- **Number of bedrooms:** You must put the number of bedrooms the property has as readers will then know if your property can accommodate them.

- **Price:** In any advert, you must put the price. I always quote a weekly rent; for example, £80 per week. This way the tenant may assume that the rent is £320 per month (thinking that there are four weeks in a month whereas there are actually 4.33 weeks in a month), when in fact it's £346 per calendar month. Your property will appear cheaper than other properties that are quoted per calendar month. If you price your property at £79 rather than £80, the impact is even more significant.

  However, do be aware not to include anything deliberately misleading as you'll be in breach of the Property Misdescriptions Act 1991.

- **Features:** If it's got a new bathroom, then say so! Anything that isn't standard with a property, such as a garage, separate dining room, large garden or new carpets, will attract more interest.

- **Telephone number:** Don't only give out your mobile number! You'll receive fewer calls as everyone knows that a five-minute call to a mobile costs a small fortune, especially to the people that you're trying to target. Put a landline down as well as a mobile. I have a freephone number which costs me 4p per minute to receive; a small price to pay to get someone talking about your property. Freephone providers are detailed in the reference chapter.

To find out about the local newspaper in the area of the property you have bought or are thinking about buying, visit www.newspapersoc.org.uk.

Through a letting agent

This is the most expensive way to find a tenant. He usually charges one month's rent plus VAT. But he will show prospective tenants round, run credit checks, ask for references, arrange a standing order and do an inventory check on the property. I would recommend this if you work or live far away from the property.

If you can't let the property

If you're having trouble letting the property, there are a number of things you can do. I suggest you take action in the following order:

Action	Why?
Reduce the rent.	If you can't let it out at the price you want, then reduce the rent. It's the basic economics of supply and demand. I suggest reducing the rent by £2 per week increments.
Widen the criteria for the type of tenant wanted.	If you've asked for non-smokers, then consider smokers. The smell can be eradicated quite easily by a local cleaning company if need be.
Accept a tenant without a deposit.	A letting agent would be horrified by this advice. However, I've done this on a number of occasions, especially for DSS claimants who simply don't have that kind of cash to pay. I recommend this approach for properties that are not in the best of condition, and where the tenant is a family and are currently on benefits so the claim will go through smoothly. You have to ask yourself whether the tenant can do any more damage to the property considering its current state. Most people are looking for a place they can call home rather than moving into somewhere with the intention of wrecking it three months down the line.

Action	Why?
Furnish the property.	This will be expensive and it's no guarantee that the place will attract tenants. Consider it if you're getting calls rejecting the property because it's unfurnished.
Sell it!	This is a drastic measure as I think any property in the UK is lettable – it's simply the rent you're asking for that will deter possible tenants. However, if you're experiencing trouble letting it, get out! Sell it and buy something else.

Credit checking your tenants

You can check the credit of your tenant like a lender credit checks a borrower. This costs between £10 and £94, depending on what service you require. Some credit-checking agencies guarantee the rent if your tenant defaults. All letting agents insist that landlords do this, but I disagree. Credit checks are advisable for only certain types of tenants and areas. Let me explain by way of a table detailing the different types of tenant (private or DSS) and area (low and high demand for rental properties). A 'Yes' in the box means that you should credit check your tenant.

		Tenant	
		Private	**Benefit claimant**
Area	High demand for rental property	Yes	No
	Low demand for rental property	No	No

So only in one out of four circumstances would you normally obtain a credit check on your prospective tenant. The justification for this is as follows:

- **Private tenant in high demand area:** The tenant is paying all the rent and you can afford to be choosy as there is high demand for your property, so it's therefore worth credit checking. This ensures that you get the best tenant. I would strongly advise you to get an employer's reference as confirmation that the company employs him and to use the credit check as only a supporting tool.

- **Private tenant in low demand:** If you've had few calls for your property and you wish to have only a private tenant, then you cannot be choosy. Most people will fail a credit check – even I do. I am a chartered accountant, but I have a default that I'm currently investigating from 18 months ago for £4.89, which renders my credit check as a failure. So a credit check doesn't always guarantee the best tenant; it can only support the tenant's case. That's why it's important to get an employer's reference.

- **DSS tenant in high demand:** The council pays the majority of the rent, so there is no point credit checking a tenant for, say, a £10-a-week top-up. The tenant would probably fail the check anyway.

- **DSS tenant in low demand:** The same reason as above.

Credit checking is also dependent on your risk factor. If you're a risk-averse investor (risk factor 1), then it's probably advisable to get the full credit check that guarantees the rent, if the tenant fails. If you're willing to accept some degree of risk (risk factors 2–6), then it's advisable to get a credit check in the circumstances noted above. If you're a risk-taker (risk factor 7) like me, then never get a credit check. Get an employer's reference. (See chapter 1 for more information on risk factors.)

I use my common sense and intuition; it hasn't failed me yet. A prospective tenant who fails a credit check could be better than a tenant who passes a credit check. Let me explain. The two most common causes for someone to fail a credit check, even though their credit rating is still good, are:

1. **The tenant has never had credit:** Just because someone has never had credit doesn't make them uncreditworthy. For example, you may have a university graduate looking to move into your property as he has just got his first job in the area. He may be from a good family who will bail him out if he gets into any money problems. One would imagine that he is responsible enough to take the financial

commitment of a tenancy, considering he has gone to university. He will probably be earning in excess of the national average wage and will be able to afford the rent comfortably. Taking these factors on board, he may still fail a credit check. However, he may be the most suitable tenant for your property after taking everything into consideration.

2. **Low value defaults:** I have a default for £4.89 as mentioned above. I would fail some credit checks because of this. A £4.89 default doesn't make me uncreditworthy under any circumstances. You have to look at the tenant's situation as a whole, rather than whether he passes or fails a credit check. Don't be afraid to ask what he earns and compare that to the rent you're charging. If the monthly rent is approximately one-third of his monthly income, then he can probably afford it.

The most common causes for a tenant to pass a credit check but ultimately end up defaulting are:

1. **The tenant loses his job:** No amount of credit checking can predict this.

2. **The tenant's household splits up:** When couples split up, their financial commitments are the last to get a look-in. If you've let to a group of students and one of them leaves, it can then be very difficult to chase him or to get the rest of the household to make up the difference. Just because a tenant passes a credit check now doesn't mean that he will honour his commitments in the future. His circumstances have now changed – this is why people default!

3. **The tenant misbudgeted:** If this is the first time the tenant has ever taken on the responsibility of occupying and paying for a home, then it's possible that the tenant has miscalculated or omitted some of the other costs associated with running a home. Add in rates, Council Tax, electricity, etc., and the tenant quickly falls in arrears. Ask the tenant if he has ever run his own household and ascertain if the tenant is aware of all the costs involved in doing so.

So you can see that credit checks have limited use. The key questions you need to be asking yourself about the prospective tenant is:

• Can he afford it now and in the future?

• Has he got a temporary or permanent job?

- Has he got a supportive family and can you get them to be guarantors for the rent?

- Does he appear to know all the costs involved in running a household?

I assume that if someone can afford to pay more than a month's deposit and one week's rent in advance, then he will probably be able to pay the rent in the future. So far I've not been very wrong; the time I've been wrong is when I've not taken a deposit and let a tenant move in with just one week's rent in advance. The tenant quickly falls into arrears because he cannot budget. That is why he never had a deposit in the first place!

Dealing with councils for housing benefit payments (DSS)

If you decide to accept someone on benefits, then the local council will pay most of the rent. Many investors don't like DSS tenants, but I've had little trouble with them and once set up, the rent simply arrives at your doorstep. There are a number of key factors when dealing with the DSS:

- **You'll get paid four weeks in arrears:** All councils pay four weeks in arrears. If cash flow is crucial, then don't take on DSS. Initially the council invariably will take between four weeks and 16 weeks to pay. This is because you depend on the tenant providing all the information that the council requires. To help speed up the process, ensure that the application goes in long before the tenant moves into the property. Also, make sure that the original tenancy agreement and other original documents are sent to the housing benefit office promptly. Tenants should be asked to sign a letter of authority authorising the housing benefit office to provide information to the landlord. If the tenant is slow to respond to the council, consider issuing notices of eviction to the tenant to hurry him up.

- **Ensure that the benefit cheques get paid directly to you:** All housing benefit can be paid directly to the landlord if the tenant signs a consent form. It's a must if you take on DSS tenants. This way you get paid directly by the council and you avoid the tenants pocketing the cash.

- **Claw-backs:** If the rent from the housing benefit office is paid directly to you, you can present yourself with a potential problem that if the housing benefit office discovers that an overpayment of benefit has been made to a previous landlord of the tenant, it can deduct the overpayment from rent paid to you. To protect yourself, check out your tenants carefully and, if possible, obtain a reference from the previous landlord. However, under new regulations which came into effect in October 2001, if you report (in writing) your suspicion of your tenant being fraudulent, the local authority will not claw-back from you, provided that you haven't colluded with the tenant in obtaining the overpayment.

The relationship between landlord and tenant

Your tenant isn't your friend! If your friend approaches you wishing to live in one of your properties, then say no – make some excuse. We all know the feeling when we've lent a friend £20 on a night out and we then have to ask for the money back; we all hate doing it. There is a good reason why we don't like doing so and that is because money and friends don't mix. Many friends in the past have fallen out over very small amounts of money, let alone a month's rent.

If your tenant tries to become friendly with you, by inviting you to his Christmas party, for instance, always decline. The relationship between landlord and tenant is strictly a business relationship and if this becomes blurred, then you're heading for trouble. This doesn't mean you have to be overly distant. Remember that you're in business with each other and that is the only reason why you know each other. For the relationship to last, the following simple contract needs to hold – you're supplying a safe property for the tenant to live in and the tenant is paying you the rent on time. Don't complicate matters by drifting into a friendship/business relationship.

Rent collection

You can collect your rent in four main ways:

1. Using a letting agent

2. Via your bank

3. Through the post

4. Face-to-face

Apart from using a letting agent, the way to collect the rent should be dictated by the tenant. You need to make the way the tenant pays his rent as easy as possible and this will be determined by the tenant. Your choice of tenant shouldn't be dictated by the ease of collection of rent. The choice of tenant should be dictated by the factors mentioned above. It's your duty to work around the tenant if you want the right tenant and to receive the rent on time.

Using a letting agent

Letting agents can handle the whole process of letting your property. This involves finding a tenant, taking inventories, collecting or guaranteeing rent and dealing with all tenant and property problems – sounds too good to be true. However, letting agents are expensive! For a full management service the fee charged can range from 12 to 20 per cent plus VAT of the rent collected. We accountants call this 'top line commission'. It's called this because the letting agents are charging commission on the rental income rather than the overall profit you're making. The expression 'top line' comes from the fact that income is the top line in any profit or loss account.

An agent's fee can wipe out a significant proportion of the profit you potentially could make. Look at this following example, where method 1 is with an agent and method 2 is without an agent:

£		
	Method 1	**Method 2**
Rental income	400	400
Mortgage	(200)	(200)
Building insurance	(10)	(10)
Sundry expenses	(10)	(10)
Agent's fee (15% + VAT)	(70)	Nil
Net profit	110	180

We can see that a 15 per cent agent's fee can reduce your net profit by 40 per cent – basically just under halving the profit you would make if you didn't have an agent! That isn't to say that you shouldn't use an agent. You need to decide how involved you wish to be in the day-to-day running of the property you've just bought. I would use an agent in the following circumstances:

1. **You work full-time:** This isn't to say that you shouldn't try without the help of an agent. I have a few properties that I've never seen since I first let them or I haven't spoken to the tenant since I first met him. This is because the tenant's rent is paid directly into my bank account by standing order, nothing has gone wrong with the flat since I bought it and I get workmen to do the annual inspections. In this situation, who needs an agent? Only use an agent once letting your property has eaten into your leisure time or you've just simply got fed up. You don't want your tenant ringing you up complaining of a blocked drain when you're in the middle of an important meeting!

2. **The property is far away:** If a property is more than three hours' travel away, then it's probably better to use an agent. The gross yield must be very good, though; I would say 24 per cent should be the minimum, if not higher. This is because you're using an agent and if you were only receiving a 12 per cent yield, after agent's fees, you would be making a loss.

When I first started I used an agent, as I worked full-time and didn't want to get bothered at work when something went wrong. Sometimes it can be very time-consuming chasing your tenant for rent. Remember, letting agents are experts in handling tenants and cannot do only what you do, but they can do it better; that's their business!

The only time I use an agent now is for my properties in Norton, Middlesbrough, which are at least four hours away from me by car. The rental yield on these properties is around 70 per cent! I can afford to use an agent when the profit margin is so high.

I would advise you to use an Association of Residential Letting Agents (ARLA)-accredited agent, as you're then insured against frauds committed by, and bankruptcy of, the agent. This means that you would receive all the rents collected by the agent even if the rents were not handed over by him. Proof of the fraud wouldn't be needed as the rents are covered by an insurance scheme backed by ARLA. ARLA agents can be found by visiting www.arla.co.uk.

STANDING ORDER SET-UP

PAYER

Name:	*Put the tenant's full name here*
Branch:	*Put the tenant's bank branch and full address*
A/C number:	*Put the tenant's account number here*
Sort code:	*Put the tenant's bank branch's sort code here*

PAYEE

Name:	*Put your full name here*
Branch:	*Put your bank branch and full address*
A/C number:	*Put your account number here*
Sort code:	*Put your bank branch's sort code here*

PAYMENT DETAILS

Amount:	*Put the weekly or monthly rent here*
Transfer date:	*Put the first date you want the transfer to occur here*
Repeat:	*Put the frequency either weekly or monthly here*
Last transfer date:	*Always put 'To be notified in writing'*

Please could you set up the above standing order on my behalf as soon as possible, to ensure that the first transfer payment is paid on time.

Date _____   Signed (the tenant) _____

Print Name _____

Please now send on to the payer's bank branch.

Fig 4.1 Standing order set-up

Via your bank

Assuming that your tenant has a bank account, you can set up a standing order that deposits the rent directly to your bank account from the tenant's bank account. I suggest that you use the template on page 53 and ensure that it's sent to the tenant's bank branch at the time of the tenant signing the lease. This template will set up the standing order.

Another way you can collect rent through your bank is to ask the tenant to give you a series of post-dated cheques to cover the rent. So, for example, if he is to pay a rent of £400 on the first day of the month, then ask for six cheques for £400 dated the first of the month for the next six months. You then simply present these cheques when the cheques' dates become valid.

You could also give your tenant a paying-in book for your bank account. This is best for tenants who earn cash but don't have a bank account. This way the tenant could visit your branch and deposit the rent when possible, rather than you both organising a rendezvous for the tenant to hand over the cash.

Through the post

I receive the majority of my rent through the post. This is either from the tenant himself or from the council's housing benefit departments. I prefer this method as it's easier to keep a mental check of who is supposed to be paying (because a cheque physically lands at your door on a regular basis), rather than me continually checking your bank account.

I have one tenant who consistently sends me the rent cheque by recorded delivery. As I'm never up when the postman knocks on my door (around 8am), I have to go to the sorting office to get my cheque. I asked my tenant not to send it by recorded delivery but he prefers to do it that way, so I have to accept that I have to go to the sorting office every week! Remember, the tenant always dictates the method of payment.

Under no circumstances should you allow the tenant to pay cash through the post.

Face-to-face

It's unlikely that the tenant will insist on face-to-face collection of the rent. You may feel more comfortable collecting the rent face-to-face so you can see what state the property is being kept in. If the tenant is happy with you collecting the rent that way, it's important that you don't let him feel that you're checking up on him. This will make him feel uncomfortable and it could lead to him moving out. If you've chosen the right tenant, you won't need to check up on him so often and you can revert to the payment method that suits the tenant.

Minimising void periods

There are five key ways to minimise the time between the old tenant leaving and the new tenant entering:

1. Neutral decoration

2. Invest in high demand areas

3. Be less fussy!

4. Invest in a property for which there is high demand

5. Advertise the property in adequate time

Neutral decoration

This is simply common sense. If the property has been decorated in a feminine way, such as flowery borders and pink colours, then you're already cutting out half the market: the boys! If the property has been decorated to a specific taste, such as chintz, then you're going to exclude tenants who don't like chintz.

You have to make your property suitable for the widest range of tenants. Ensure that the decoration is neutral and not personalised. Tenants personalise their properties with their possessions. You have to rely on luck, if you don't neutralise the decoration, that the right tenant turns up when the property becomes available to rent again.

Invest in high demand areas

My philosophy is that any property can be let out eventually. If you want to minimise the time the property is left vacant between tenants, then go for a property where you know demand is high for rented properties. A local letting agent will be able to tell you this. Also, you can speak to the accommodation projects listed in the reference chapter or you can place a rogue advert in the local paper and see how many calls you get.

Investing in high demand areas has a cost. It's probable that high demand areas will have higher property purchase prices than a low demand area. This will affect your yield but remember, don't break the rule of 12! You'll also be competing against other landlords so you'll have to be able to move on the purchase quickly; have your finance in place.

Be less fussy!

If you're excluding a certain type of tenant, then you run the risk of having a void period. The more prospective tenants you exclude, the greater the likelihood of the property being vacant. If you're relying on your strict perception of the right tenant to appear around the time your existing tenant decides to leave, then you're relying heavily on luck.

Ways of becoming less fussy without compromising too much on the quality of tenant are:

- **Consider non-professional tenants.** There is nothing to say a professional is any better than a hard-working builder as a tenant, so don't advertise for 'professionals only'.

- **Consider pets.** You could consider cats but no dogs, or accept only caged pets. What damage could a goldfish do?

- **Consider DSS.** I have no problem with DSS claimants. You could just consider claimants on Incapacity Benefit rather than Jobseeker's Allowance.

Invest in a property for which there is high demand

As mentioned elsewhere, a two-bedroom ex-local authority property generally covers a high percentage of prospective tenants. If there is high demand for a certain type of property, then invest in that type of property. Currently there is high demand for private two-bedroom flats in London because there is less stigma now for professionals to share. Again, there will be high demand for these properties from investors and private people and this will drive the purchase price up, consequently affecting your yield.

Advertise the property in adequate time

Your existing tenant has to give you sufficient notice if he wishes to vacate the property, usually of one month. This gives you ample time to find a tenant. If you've had a good relationship with your tenant, he will probably not mind showing prospective tenants around during his one-month notice period.

As soon as you do get notice, then follow the instructions given in this chapter for advertising for a tenant. There is no point in hanging around, as the longer you leave it the less time you have to find one.

However, do remember that by law a landlord must not sign a new tenancy agreement until the existing tenant has moved out. Otherwise, you'll be in breach of contract.

CHAPTER 5

Expanding your portfolio

OK, so I've told you how to get one property. But how do you get 50 properties in five years? The key is remortgaging. Remortgaging is all about releasing the equity that's locked up in the property that you currently own.

So if you've bought your first property for £50,000 and you can get it revalued in excess of £70,000, then you can access some of that £20,000 equity to buy further properties. It's this release of equity that enables you to buy further properties, as this equity can be used as deposits for further properties.

The revaluation trick

I bought a property in June 2001 for £23,500 in Northampton with a £6,000 deposit, did nothing to it, got it revalued at £42,000 by a different lender four months later, released £18,000, used this for further deposits and bought four more properties! In effect, one property enabled me to get four further properties. This is possible if you watch out for these bargains.

The reason a £23,500 property can be revalued at £42,000 is that when you get a revaluation the valuer is only giving an opinion on what the property is worth and it's only a guide. However, the mortgage company takes this as the market value to lend against.

When filling out the form for a remortgage never be conservative about what you think the property is worth. If you bought it for £23,500, say it's worth double that, like I did (£47,000) and the valuer may come back at £42,000. This actually happened. This way you can raise the maximum amount of the cheapest borrowings to buy further properties.

I know the effective mortgage payment increases when you remortgage, but the additional properties you buy and the income these further generate more than compensate for the increased mortgage payment. Let me show you by way of example:

Rob buys his first property two years ago for £60,000 with a 25 per cent deposit.

Property 1	
Rental	£600
Mortgage (at 6%)	£225
Profit	£375
Valuation	£60,000
Borrowings	£45,000

If an application is made that revalues the property at £85,000 and the lender is willing to lend 85 per cent, then the funds that can be raised are:

£85,000 x 85 per cent minus £45,000 = £27,250

With this £27,250, Rob can buy three further properties for £60,000 each placing £9,000 deposit each (3 x £9,000 = £27,000), but the original mortgage payment has gone up on property 1 due to the extra borrowings:

Property	1	2	3	4	Total
Rental £	600	600	600	600	2,400
Mortgage £ (6%)	361	255	255	255	1,126
Profit £	239	345	345	345	1,274

So, by a combination of revaluing, releasing equity due to increased borrowings and the purchase of further investment properties, Rob's profit has nearly trebled from £375 to £1,274. This is because the equity Rob has released, borrowed at six per cent, generates income far in excess of six per cent due to the purchase of three investment properties. The profit generated from these three further properties covers the additional interest cost of remortgaging the original property and an extra £899!

Don't be worried if the revaluation breaks the rule of 12, i.e. the property gets revalued to £85,000 but you're only getting £600 per month rental. Remember, borrowing is cheap, so if you can get borrowings at six per cent to get a return in excess of 20 per cent on property, then do it. Only hesitate from doing this when borrowing rates are in excess of returns that can be had from the property.

Risk analysis for the future

This section deals with things that can go wrong. When you're in business you're always susceptible to going bust. It happened to Railtrack, so it can happen to you! What makes a successful business isn't only the ability to make a profit and generate cash but to continue to do so. This means being able to:

1. react to changing market conditions quickly;

2. protect against threats to your long-term income.

React to changing market conditions quickly

The profit you generate is dependent on two basic elements: rental income and mortgage expenditure. If either of these elements changes in your favour (market rental income increases or market mortgage expenditure decreases), then you're stupid not to capitalise on this. You need to keep your eye on the market for both these elements. The easiest way to do this is:

- **Rental income:** Simply scan the 'accommodation to let' adverts in the local paper once every two months or so and see what a similar property to the one you own is going for. If the market value rent has risen for your property, then increase your rent accordingly when you're able to do so. You're able to do this after the duration of the lease has expired.

- **Mortgage expenditure:** If you're on a fixed rate and interest rates are dropping, then consider remortgaging at a lower rate. Approach your lender initially and tell it that you're considering remortgaging and it may even reduce the rate – it's worth a try.

The more money you make by keeping abreast of changing market conditions, the more you've set aside for further reinvestment, hence further profit.

Protect against threats to your long-term income

The key to managing risk in the long-term is diversification – 'not putting all your eggs in one basket'. The way to do this is to vary the following factors when investing in property:

- **Area:** Try to invest in different towns and cities. Rental demand or property price changes can vary according to area due to significant increases in crime rates, redundancies, pollution, etc.

- **Property:** Buy both private and ex-local authority properties. Consider both flats and houses. Don't stick exclusively to two-bedroom properties; consider studios and four-bedroom properties. This way you're not stuck with seeking a particular type of tenant.

- **Tenant:** Consider both DSS and private tenants.

- **Borrowings:** Go for a mixture of fixed and variable borrowings. Don't stick exclusively with one lender.

The table on page 63 details the threats to your long-term income and how diversification minimises the impact of the threat. This isn't an exhaustive list. These are just some of the threats that I've faced but I've been able to weather them due to diversification.

Threat	Effect of diversification
Interest rates increase dramatically	Because some of your borrowings are fixed, the increase in interest rates will not fully impact on your mortgage cost. How risk-averse you are will depend on the ratio of fixed to variable borrowings. Even if you're of risk factor 7, I still recommend that you fix some of your borrowings cost.
Demand for rental properties in the area falls significantly	This could be due to heavy job losses in the area. As you have properties in other areas, the impact of the job losses isn't felt on the whole portfolio. If this does happen, the key is to cover just your mortgage payment until demand picks up. If you drop your rent to an attractive price, just above your mortgage payment, you'll ensure that you'll get a tenant before most other landlords. If it's unlikely that demand will pick up, then consider selling.
Changes in housing benefit entitlement	Some councils have cut back on housing benefit and insist that the tenant contributes more to the rent. The tenant usually struggles to do this. If you've invested in different areas, your portfolio isn't subject to one council change. Also, if you've taken on a combination of private and DSS tenants, then the impact is lessened.

Table 5.1 Threats and effects of diversification

Property crashes and how to avoid them

No one can tell you with any great certainty how to avoid a property crash. This is because nobody can really see more than three to six months ahead of the indices that affect property prices.

What I can do is tell you what these indices are, why they affect property prices and how you can track these indices so you can make a judgement on which way prices are going to go.

Now, let's first define what a property crash is. We can all be certain that a crash is a fall in prices, but by how much? Is it one per cent, five per cent, 25 per cent or 50 per cent? There is no clear definition. The media would have you believe a five per cent fall is a crash as 'house price crash' headlines sell newspapers! However, based on my business experience, a fall of 20 per cent plus, sustained for more than six months, would be a crash in my books. It has to be a significant percentage and 20 per cent is!

Now I know 15 per cent is as well, but we're talking about a crash here and even though 15 per cent is significant, I think a 20 per cent dent in your wealth would hurt. A threshold has to be set and I believe that it could take over five years to recover a 20 per cent loss.

The drop in prices has to be sustained. So if prices dropped 20 per cent in three months and recover in the next three months, then it's not a crash but merely a blip. So really one should only fear a 20 per cent fall in prices for a sustained period of over six months.

So what are the key indices that prop property prices up? There are four key indices or factors that determine property prices:

Indice/ Factor	Description	Why
Interest rates	The borrowing rate being charged to homeowners who have borrowed to buy their property.	The size of the interest rate affects borrowing rates, which then determine a homeowner's monthly mortgage payment. If this becomes too high, properties become unaffordable, homeowners are forced to sell, a flood of properties enter the market and it becomes a buyer's market. Property prices are bid heavily down as the homeowner has to sell.

Indice/ Factor	Description	Why
Liquidity purchase	The availability of finance to make a property purchase.	Properties are bought with the bank's money. If this money dries up, there is no money for potential property purchasers to buy these properties. Effectively, properties could be bought only for cash and then prices could only ever be what is available in the individual's bank account.
Unemployment rates	The amount of people unemployed.	Mortgages have to be serviced by wages. If everyone became unemployed, there would be no wages to service the mortgage and hence property prices would fall dramatically.
Fiscal policy	The taxation regime which taxes income earned by individuals.	Mortgages are paid for with wages where the tax has already been deducted (called 'net pay'). If tax was to increase, net pay would decrease and then reduce the ability for a homeowner to meet his monthly mortgage payment.

There are other factors but the four above are the four real key factors you should be aware of. The data you should follow to track these factors are:

Indice/ Factor	Data	Why
Interest rates	MPC meetings Inflation rates	Check the Monetary Policy Committee's meeting notes

Indice/ Factor	Data	Why
		and votes. If there is a 5-4 vote in favour of keeping rates on hold, it could be that next month is a 4-5 vote the other way! Also, check inflation rates to see that they are within the government's targets. If there has been three months where it has exceeded targets, then a rate increase is likely.
Liquidity	Financial press Council of Mortgage Lenders' report	The press comments regularly on how loose or tight the banks are. Also, the Council of Mortgage Lenders gives precise figures of overall lending. Check whether lending is increasing or decreasing each quarter to spot if banks are getting jittery.
Unemployment rates	Unemployment rate	This is a government official figure. It's announced once a month and can be found from the government's own official National Statistics website (www.statistics.gov.uk).
Fiscal policy	Chancellor's Budget	Tax gets reviewed in March every year. If there is a heavy increase in VAT or Income Tax, then expect this to hurt homeowners when the increase kicks in. Also, look out for the hidden taxes which can sometimes hurt even more!

CHAPTER 6

Tax

We all hate paying tax, but we cannot ignore it. This chapter deals with the key figures when calculating your tax and how legally to minimise your tax bill. Let's identify the types of tax you'll be subject to if you invest in property.

Types of tax

There are two types of tax that property is subject to:

1. **Income Tax:** This tax is applied to the profit generated from the renting out of the property. It has to be paid every year in half-yearly instalments on 31 January and 31 July. Taxable profit is deemed to be taxable rental income minus allowable expenditure.

    Taxable rental income and, more importantly, allowable expenditure will be defined in detail in this chapter so you can easily calculate and reduce your taxable profit by claiming all allowable expenditure.

2. **Capital Gains Tax:** This tax is only applied once the property has been sold. It's essentially the tax applied to the profit you've made from selling the property.

    Detailed below are certain reliefs that you can claim to minimise your Capital Gains Tax bill to zero!

Income Tax

You'll only ever pay tax on your taxable profits, that is to say you have to make money before you pay tax. Income has to exceed expenditure; if you've not achieved this, you shouldn't even be interested in this chapter. If you're in the position where income does exceed expenditure, then read on.

The equation

The simple equation for calculating your Income Tax bill is:

Taxable rental income minus allowable expenditure = taxable profit

So in order for your taxable profit to be the lowest possible, then the 'taxable rental income' must be minimised and the 'allowable expenditure' must be maximised.

Minimising 'taxable rental income'

This is very difficult to do. Taxable rental income is deemed to be any rental income earned in the period, with the period usually being the tax year 6 April to 5 April. 'Earned' means not only what the tenant has paid, but also what the tenant owes even if the money hasn't yet been paid. Basically, there are no tricks in reducing taxable rental income, apart from one: if a tenant is 14 days in arrears, you can consider that debt as a bad debt and not include it as taxable rental income. If the tenant does end up paying, you can include the income in the following accounting period. 14 days' outstanding rent is in real terms not that much and you'll have to pay tax on the income in the following year anyway. The only real benefit is cash flow. This is because you save slightly on your tax bill and defer payment on this omitted rental income until your next tax return the following year.

Maximising 'allowable expenditure'

This is easier to do than minimising rental income. This is because HM Revenue & Customs grants certain allowances based on certain definitions, as well as allowable expenditure. This means expenditure and allowances can be deducted from the taxable rental income to derive the taxable profit. The two pure definitions that you need to remember for allowable expenditure and taxable allowances, as stated by HM Revenue & Customs, are:

1. 'Any costs you incur for the sole purposes of earning business profits'

2. 'Capital allowances on the cost of buying a capital asset, or a wear-and-tear allowance for furnished lettings'

'Any costs you incur for the sole purposes of earning business profits'

Any expense you incur 'wholly, necessarily and exclusively' for the business is fully deductible from your rental income. Any personal expenditure that you make that relates to the business is partly tax deductible from your income. To make sure that you include all expenses that are allowable against your rental income, refer to the following checklists of expenses for inclusion in your Tax Return:

Fully tax deductible expenses:

Expense	Description
Repairs and maintenance	All repairs and maintenance costs are fully tax deductible. Where the property has been altered so extensively that it's deemed to be reconstructed the property is then considered to be 'modified' rather than 'repaired', hence no amount of the expense is allowed. The only amount allowed would be the estimated cost of maintenance or repair made unnecessary by the modification. Examples of repairs and maintenance expenditure that are fully tax deductible are: • Painting and decoration • Damp treatment • Roof repairs • Repairs to goods supplied with the property (e.g. a washing machine)

Expense	Description
Finance charges	Any interest you pay on a loan that you took out to acquire a property is fully tax deductible. It's only the interest and not the capital repayment part that is tax deductible. If any of the finance raised (the loan) is used for personal use, such as a holiday, then the interest paid on the amount paid for the holiday isn't tax deductible. The typical interest payments that are allowed are: • Interest on the mortgage taken out to get the property • Interest on any secured or unsecured loans taken out to get the property Arrangement fees charged by a lender are also tax deductible. Interest paid on the car you use to run the property business is partly tax deductible – see below.
Legal and professional fees	Allowable expenditure is: • Letting agent's fees for the collection in rent, including the VAT (unless you're VAT-registered) • Legal fees for evicting tenants • Accountancy fees for preparing your accounts Disallowable expenditure is: • Surveyor's fees initially paid out to value the property (unless the survey was unsuccessful and you never acquired the property, in which case it's a fully deductible expense) • Legal fees incurred through the purchase of the property When it comes to calculating the capital gain when you sell the property, these expenses are added to the purchase price. The capital gain is calculated as follows: Gain = selling price minus purchase price

Expense	Description
	This results in the purchase price being higher than the actual price paid because of the addition of initial professional fees. So the taxable gain is lower. These fees are subject to full indexation, as is the purchase price, to allow for price inflation – see 'Capital Gains Tax' below. So, at the time of writing, you do get some tax relief but only further down the line when you sell the property.
Council Tax, electricity, water and gas	If you're renting out all the rooms, all the usual running costs involved with a property are fully tax deductible. This assumes that none of the tenants make a contribution to the bills. If you let out your property inclusive of all the bills, then you can fully charge all the bills you include with the rent. If you let out your property exclusive of all bills (which is the usual way), then you cannot claim. Remember, you can only claim the expense if you actually paid it!
Insurance	• Buildings insurance • Contents insurance • Rental guarantee Insurance premiums are fully tax deductible. Life assurance premiums are not, as this is personal expenditure. Car insurance is, but only partly – see below.
Advertising	Any advertising costs in connection with finding a tenant or selling your property are fully tax deductible. This includes: • Newspaper adverts • Agent's commission
Ground rent	This is the rent you pay if you own a leasehold flat, typically a nominal amount of £50 per annum.
Service charges	Service charges are incurred if you own a leasehold flat. If you pay these charges, then they are fully tax deductible.

Expense	Description
Letting agent's fees	Any fee that is charged by a letting agent is fully tax deductible, apart from any fees charged for leases created for longer than a year. If a fee is charged for creating a five-year lease, only one-fifth of the fee can be charged for each year.
Stationery	Any stationery costs incurred in connection with running your property business are fully tax deductible. This will include items such as: • All paper and envelopes • Postage • All printing expenditure

Partly tax deductible expenses:

Expense	Description
Motor expenses	Motor costs are allowable, but only when your car is used in connection with the property business. It's up to you to decide how much time you think you spend using your car for private use and business use. It has to be reasonable. Once you've decided on the split of personal to business, say 70% personal, 30% business, you can charge the business percentage against your taxable rental income, in this case 30%. Typical motor expenses are: • Car insurance • Fuel • Servicing and repairs • Interest paid on the loan taken out to acquire the car A fraction of the purchase price of the car can also be taken into account as an allowance – see below. I charge 80% of my motor expenses to the business. This is because I have 50 properties to maintain around the country and I spend 80% of my driving time on business engagements.

Expense	Description
Telephone calls	Again, this is like motor expenses. If you spend 30% of your time on the phone in connection with your business, then charge 30% of:
	• Total landline call charges
	• Total line rental for your landline
	• Total mobile call charges
	• Total line rental for your mobile
	If there are obvious large private calls (say in excess of £5), then exclude these from the total call expense when calculating the 30% charge. If you have a fax line, then charge 100% of fax expenses as it's easy to convince HM Revenue & Customs that you own a fax machine for business use!

Again, this isn't an exhaustive list. To make sure you legally maximise your allowable taxable expenditure, you have to remember the following two principles:

- Include expenditure if it's 'wholly, necessarily and exclusively' needed for the business. If it is, include it. If it's not, exclude it or partly include it.

- Include a proportional amount of expenditure that is split between business and personal such as motor expenses and telephone calls.

'Capital allowances on the cost of buying a capital asset, or a wear-and-tear allowance for furnished lettings'

This basically means that you can either charge:

- 100 per cent of the cost of any asset used to furnish the property, or

- Ten per cent of the rent

as a tax-deductible expense. You cannot do both. I would always recommend doing the latter, charging ten per cent of the rent, because once you opt to do one or the other, you cannot change for the duration of your business. The reason I recommend ten per cent of the rent is because ten per cent of the rent is likely to be greater than 100 per cent of the cost of the asset. If this isn't the case now, it will probably be in the future. It's better to suffer the lower deductible expense now for the benefit in the future.

You can still claim capital allowances for any asset that you use in the business, such as motor vehicles, but it will be restricted to the business element only. So, in the example above of the motor vehicle with 30 per cent business use, a car used in the business costing £5,000 would attract the following relief:

30 per cent x 25 per cent x £5,000 = £375.

You can never charge the cost of an item that you intend to use for longer than one year against your rental income. Anything purchased for use longer than one year is deemed to be an asset and only 25 per cent of the cost can be charged each year.

Capital Gains Tax

This tax only arises when you sell the property. The capital gain is worked out as:

Sale price minus purchase price minus indexation allowance/taper relief = capital gain

The sale price is deemed to be the price achieved after deducting estate agent's costs, solicitor's fees and any other expenses that were incurred wholly, necessarily and exclusively in the sale of the property.

The purchase price is the cost of the property, plus all survey and legal costs.

Indexation allowance and taper relief

Up until 5 April 1998, you were allowed to set against any capital gain the element of that profit which was caused by inflation. In other words, you didn't have to pay tax on inflationary gains. This amount, called indexation, was calculated by working out the amount the retail price of the house had increased between the date of purchase and the date of sale.

Since 6 April 1998, indexation has no longer been an allowable deduction. However, you can still claim it, but it can only be calculated from the gain acquired before 5 April 1998.

The government, instead, have now introduced taper relief, which came into effect on 5 April 1998. According to the number of completed years that the asset has been owned after that date, only a percentage of the gain will be chargeable. This relief is very complicated to calculate and as a result, I strongly advise you to take professional advice or see if HM Revenue & Customs can process your query quickly.

How to reduce your capital gain

The calculation

The way to reduce your capital gain is to understand the capital gain calculation. If you dispose of a property, the following calculation will be made to work out your capital gain:

Sales price minus purchase price minus allowable costs = capital gain

The sales price and the purchase price are fixed. You cannot change what you sold the property for or what you paid for it.

Allowable costs

To reduce your capital gain you have to maximise the allowable costs. The allowable costs you can include, from HM Revenue & Customs' Capital Gains Help Sheet, are:

- Solicitor's costs
- Accountancy fees
- Mortgage broker's fees
- Redemption penalties on cleared mortgages
- Stamp duty
- Advertising
- Estate agent's fees
- Valuations needed to calculate your gain

- Any improvements that still need doing to the property
- Legal costs in defending your title to the property

So the first part of reducing your capital gain is to include ALL costs involved with the purchase, ownership period and sale of the property that fall within the definitions stated by HM Revenue & Customs. But it doesn't stop here! You can get further relief on the gain.

Personal allowance

Everybody gets a Capital Gains Tax allowance of £9,200 per tax year (2007/08 figure) rising year on year with inflation. So if you have a gain of £10,000, then it's reduced by £9,200 to £800.

If you're selling a couple of properties, you can straddle the sales either side of the 5 April year end date of the tax year. This way you can apply your capital gains allowance for the tax year prior to 5 April on one of the properties and your capital gains allowance for the tax year after 5 April for the other property. This way you can make full use of your yearly allowances.

There is one final trick – your principal place of residence.

Principal place of residence (PPR)

Your own personal residence isn't liable for Capital Gains Tax, so any gain you make is all yours. If part of your strategy is to let out your home and move into another property and you sell your original home within three years of leaving it, there is no tax to pay! If you sell after the three years, you still get relief for three years. Let's look at this example:

Roger lives in a house that has been his personal place of residence for eight years, when he bought it, but he decides to move out and rent it out. If he sells it two years after he rented it out, there is no tax to pay. If he sells it five years later, only $(5-3)/13$ of the gain is chargeable.

The equation is as follows:

(Amount of years rented minus three years)/period of ownership

CHAPTER 7

Legal aspects

The legal aspects a landlord faces can be split into three broad categories:

- Contractual
- Regulatory
- All-encompassing

This chapter provides an overview of the main legal issues that face a landlord. Further in-depth discussion on landlord and tenant law can be found in Lawpack's *Residential Lettings* guide.

Contractual

'Contractual' refers to the legal contracts that you'll sign and enter into. You'll be bound to fulfil your obligations under the terms of the contract. Breach of terms can result in you being sued and ultimately paying damages to the aggrieved party. As a landlord you'll enter into legal contracts with your:

1. Lender

2. Tenant

3. Insurers

4. Letting agent

Lender

Prior to entering into a contract with a lender, it has to know about you. The lender asks you a number of questions and expects the truth. If it's discovered that you've misled the lender by any of your answers to its questions, it can demand repayment of the loan in full plus all recovery costs. It can also inform the police and charge you with obtaining finance by deception. This is fraud and you can go to prison.

Once the lender has established that you're a person worth lending to, it insists that you sign a contract. The lender sets the terms of the contract. As it has lent money to you, it's the lender's right to set the terms of the contract. Unless you're borrowing a large sum of money, then you can never include any clauses in the contract based on your terms; that's just the way it is. The key terms of the contract are:

- **Payment:** You have to pay the mortgage repayments on the dates the lender dictates. If you fail to do so, the lender can repossess the property.

- **Maintenance:** You must keep the property in a good state of repair and for it to be fit enough to be habitable.

- **Occupation:** You must not leave the property vacant for more than 30 days.

Tenant

There are several legal documents that are created when you find a suitable tenant:

1. An inventory and statement of condition
2. An Assured Shorthold Tenancy Agreement
3. An eviction order

An inventory and statement of condition

An inventory, sometimes called a statement of condition, is a document listing all items that are in the property, including their descriptions, quantities and condition. Both the tenant and the landlord should sign this list. When the tenant decides to leave the property you can check the list to see what is left in the property. If there are any deviations from the list, you can charge the tenant to correct the deviation. So, for example, if there were four dining chairs when the tenant moved in and now there are only three, you can deduct the cost of replacing the dining chair from the tenant's deposit.

If you get an inventory done, it will ensure that the tenant thinks that you care about the place you're letting and he will be less likely to damage the property. If the condition of the carpet is recorded, the tenant is more likely to remove any stains caused, as he fears that you'll deduct cleaning costs from his deposit.

The best format is to prepare the inventory on a room-to-room basis with columns for the item, condition and quality. Also, do allow space for alterations to the condition, signatures and date, plus a statement mentioning that the document is an accurate description of the property and will be used to check for any damages at the end of the tenancy.

Produce two copies – one for you and one for the tenant. It's advisable to go through the inventory with the tenant when he moves in and ensure that any alterations are made to both copies so that the documents are always identical.

To avoid any disputes, one can approach an independent company to prepare the inventory or you can download one from Lawpack's website at www.lawpack.co.uk.

An Assured Shorthold Tenancy (AST) Agreement

This is an agreement between the landlord and tenant defined by the Housing Act 1988 (which was slightly modified by the Housing Act 1996). It binds both parties to certain duties and obligations and it's only of use in England and Wales. The equivalent of an AST in Scotland is a Short Assured Tenancy (SAT).

The main features of a tenancy agreement are:

• **Rent:** How much rent is to be paid and the frequency of payment.

ASSURED SHORTHOLD TENANCY AGREEMENT

ENGLAND & WALES

Notes for Guidance

Insert date of Agreement.

DATED

Insert the address of the property to be let.

The PROPERTY
(hereinafter called 'the Property')

* Delete as applicable. The room must be identified in the Agreement.

*The DESIGNATED ROOM

* Delete as applicable. List all shared rooms in the Property.

*The SHARED PARTS

The Landlord should give here an address in England and Wales.

The LANDLORD
(hereinafter called 'the Landlord')

of ....

This is the Landlord's address for service of notices until the Tenant is notified of a different address in England and Wales.

Insert full name(s), and address(es) (if relevant) of every Tenant.

The TENANT
(hereinafter called 'the Tenant')

of ....

Where the Tenant consists of more than one person, they will all have joint and several liability under this Agreement (this means that they will each be liable for all sums due under this Agreement, not just liable for a proportionate part).

* Delete as applicable. Insert name and address of Guarantor.

*The GUARANTOR
(hereinafter called 'the Guarantor')

of ....

Insert period of Term in weeks/months and date tenancy begins.

* Delete as applicable depending on whether rent is to be paid monthly or weekly.

The TERM

.... beginning on .... **('the fixed period')**

The tenancy will then continue, still subject to the terms and conditions set out in this Agreement, from [**month to month**][**week to week**]* from the end of this fixed period unless or until the Tenant gives notice that he wishes to end the Agreement as set out in clause 4 overleaf, or the Landlord serves on the Tenant a notice under Section 21 of the Housing Act 1988, or a new form of Agreement is entered into, or this Agreement is ended by consent or a court order.

* Delete as applicable. NB If rent is paid weekly, a rent book must be provided to the tenant.

The RENT

£..................... per calendar [**month**][**week**]*

by way of standing order into the Landlord's bank, details of which have been provided to the Tenant*.

† If paid weekly, give the day in the week, e.g. Monday.

The PAYMENT DATE

The first payment to be made on the signing of this Agreement. All subsequent payments to be made [**monthly**][**weekly**]* in advance on the [.....................**day of the month**][..................... **of each week**]*†.

Further information about the Government authorised Tenancy Deposit Schemes can be obtained from their websites: The Deposit Protection Service at www.depositprotection.com, Tenancy Deposit Solutions Ltd at www.mydeposits.co.uk and The Dispute Service Ltd at www.tds.gb.com.

The DEPOSIT

£..................... which will be registered with one of the Government authorised tenancy deposit schemes ("the Tenancy Deposit Scheme") in accordance with the Tenancy Deposit Scheme Rules.

Delete this section if there is no inventory.

The INVENTORY

Being the list of the Landlord's possessions at the Property and details of condition which has been signed by the Landlord and the Tenant, a copy of which is annexed hereto.

* Delete as applicable, depending on whether whole property or room is being let.

THIS TENANCY AGREEMENT comprises the particulars detailed above and the terms and conditions printed overleaf whereby the **[Property][Designated Room, with the right to share the use of the Shared Parts with such other persons as the Landlord grants or has granted the right to use those Shared Parts]*** is hereby let by the Landlord and taken by the Tenant for the Term at the Rent.

1

This Agreement is intended to create an assured shorthold tenancy as defined in the Housing Act 1988, as amended by the Housing Act 1996, and the provisions for the recovery of possession by the Landlord in that Act apply accordingly. The Tenant understands that the Landlord will be entitled to recover possession of the Property at the end of the Term.

Delete paragraph if whole property is being let.

[Under this Agreement, the Tenant will have exclusive occupation of his Designated Room and will share with other occupiers of the Property the use of the Shared Parts of the Property .]

1. The Tenant's obligations:

1.1 To pay the Rent at the times and in the manner aforesaid.

1.2 [To pay all charges in respect of any electric, gas, water, telephonic and televisual services used at or supplied to the Property and Council Tax or any similar property tax that might be charged in addition to or replacement of it during the Term.] [To make a proportionate contribution to the costs of all charges in respect of any electric, gas, water and telephone or televisual services used at or supplied to the Property and Council Tax or any similar property tax that might be charged in addition to or replacement of it during the Term.]*

Delete sentence which does not apply.

Delete wording in square brackets that does not apply.

1.3 To keep the items on the Inventory and the interior of the [Property][Designated Room and Shared Parts]* in a good clean state and condition and not damage or injure the Property or the items on the Inventory (fair wear and tear excepted).

1.4 To yield up the [Property][Designated Room and Shared Parts]* and the items on the Inventory (if any) at the end of the Term in the same clean state and condition it/they was/were in at the beginning of the Term (but the Tenant will not be responsible for fair wear and tear caused during normal use of the Property and the items on the Inventory or for any damage covered by and recoverable under the insurance policy effected by the Landlord under clause 2.2).

1.5 Not make any alteration or addition to the Property nor without the Landlord's prior written consent (consent not to be withheld unreasonably) do any redecoration or painting of the Property.

1.6 Not do anything on or at the Property which:
1.6.1 may be or become a nuisance or annoyance to any other occupiers of the Property or owners or occupiers of adjoining or nearby premises
1.6.2 is illegal or immoral
1.6.3 may in any way affect the validity of the insurance of the Property and the items listed on the Inventory or cause an increase in the premium payable by the Landlord.

1.7 Not without the Landlord's prior consent (consent not to be withheld unreasonably) allow or keep any pet or any kind of animal at the Property.

1.8 Not use or occupy the Property in any way whatsoever other than as a private residence.

1.9 Not to assign, sublet, charge or part with or share possession or occupation of the Property (but see clause 4.1 below).

1.10 To allow the Landlord or anyone with the Landlord's written permission to enter the Property at reasonable times of the day to inspect its condition and state of repair, carry out any necessary repairs and gas inspections, or during the last month of the Term, show the Property to prospective new tenants, provided the Landlord has given 24 hours' prior written notice (except in emergency).

1.11 To pay the Landlord's reasonable costs reasonably incurred as a result of any breaches by the Tenant of his obligations under this Agreement.

1.12 To pay interest at the rate of 4% above the Bank of England base rate from time to time prevailing on any rent or other money lawfully due from the Tenant which remains unpaid for more that 14 days, interest to be paid from the date the payment fell due until payment.

1.13 To provide the Landlord with a forwarding address when the tenancy comes to an end and to remove all rubbish and all personal items (including the Tenant's own furniture and equipment) from the Property before leaving.

2. The Landlord's obligations:

2.1 The Landlord agrees that the Tenant may live in the [Property][Designated Room and Shared Parts]* without unreasonable interruption from the Landlord or any person rightfully claiming under or in trust for the Landlord.

2.2 To insure the Property and the items listed on the Inventory and use all reasonable efforts to arrange for any damage caused by an insured risk to be remedied as soon as possible and to provide a copy of the insurance policy to the Tenant if requested.

2.3 To keep in repair:
2.3.1 the structure and exterior of the Property (including drains, gutters and external pipes)
2.3.2 the installations at the Property for the supply of water, sewage, gas and electricity and for sanitation (including basins, sinks, baths and sanitary conveniences), and
2.3.3 the installations at the Property for space heating and heating water.

2.4 But the Landlord will not be required to:
2.4.1 carry out works for which the Tenant is responsible by virtue of his duty to use the Property in a tenant-like manner
2.4.2 reinstate the Property in the case of damage or destruction if the insurers refuse to pay out the insurance money due to anything the Tenant has done or failed to do
2.4.3 rebuild or reinstate the Property in the case of destruction or damage of the Property by a risk not covered by the policy of insurance effected by the Landlord.

2.5 If the property is a flat or maisonette within a larger building then the Landlord will be under similar obligations for the rest of the building but only in so far as any disrepair will affect the Tenant's enjoyment of the Property and in so far as the Landlord is legally entitled to enter the relevant part of the larger building and carry out the required works or repairs.

2.6 To arrange for the Tenant's Deposit to be protected by an authorised Tenancy Deposit Scheme in accordance with the provisions of the Housing Act 2004 within 14 days of receipt, and to comply with the rules of the Tenancy Deposit Scheme at all times.

3. Guarantor
If there is a Guarantor, he guarantees that the Tenant will keep to his obligations in this Agreement. The Guarantor agrees to pay on demand to the Landlord any money lawfully due to the Landlord by the Tenant.

4. Ending this Agreement
4.1 The Tenant cannot normally end this Agreement before the end of the Term. However, after the first

2

three months of the Term, if the Tenant can find a suitable alternative tenant, and provided this alternative tenant is acceptable to the Landlord (the Landlord's approval not to be unreasonably withheld) the Tenant may give notice to end the tenancy on a date at least one month from the date that such approval is given by the Landlord. On the expiry of such notice, provided that the Tenant pays to the Landlord the reasonable expenses reasonably incurred by the Landlord in granting the necessary approval and in granting any new tenancy to the alternative tenant, the tenancy shall end.

*Delete according to rental period.

4.2 If the Tenant stays on after the end of the fixed Term, his tenancy will continue but will run from [month to month][week to week]* (a 'periodic tenancy'). This periodic tenancy can be ended by the Tenant giving at least one month's written notice to the Landlord, the notice to expire at the end of a rental period.

4.3 If at any time

4.3.1 any part of the Rent is outstanding for 21 days after becoming due (whether formally demanded or not) and/or

4.3.2 there is any breach, non-observance or non-performance by the Tenant of any covenant or other term of this Agreement which has been notified in writing to the Tenant and the Tenant has failed within a reasonable period of time to remedy the breach and/or pay reasonable compensation to the Landlord for the breach and/or

4.3.3 any of the grounds set out as Grounds 2, 8 or Grounds 10-15 (inclusive) (which relate to breach of any obligation by a Tenant) contained in the Housing Act 1988 Schedule 2 apply

the Landlord may recover possession of the Property and this Agreement shall come to an end. The Landlord retains all his other rights in respect of the Tenant's obligations under this Agreement. Note that if anyone is living at the Property or if the tenancy is an assured or assured shorthold tenancy then the Landlord must obtain a court order for possession before re-entering the Property. This clause does not affect the Tenant's rights under the Protection from Eviction Act 1977.

5. The Deposit

5.1 The Deposit will be held in accordance with the Tenancy Deposit Scheme Rules as issued by the relevant Tenancy Deposit Scheme.

5.2 No interest will be payable to the Tenant by the Landlord in respect of the Deposit.

5.3 Subject to any relevant provisions of the Tenancy Deposit Scheme Rules, the Landlord shall be entitled to claim from the Deposit the reasonable cost of any repairs or damage to the Property or its contents caused by the Tenant (including any damage caused by the Tenant's family and visitors) and for any other financial losses suffered by the Landlord as a result of the Tenant's breach of these terms and conditions, provided the sum claimed by the Landlord is reasonably incurred and is reasonable in amount. The Landlord is not entitled to claim in respect of any damage to the Property or its contents which is due to 'fair wear and tear' i.e. which is as a result of the Tenant and his family (if any) living in the property and using it in a reasonable and lawful manner.

6. Other provisions

6.1 The Landlord hereby notifies the Tenant under Section 48 of the Landlord & Tenant Act 1987 that any notices (including notices in proceedings) should be served upon the Landlord at the address stated with the name of the Landlord overleaf.

6.2 The Landlord shall be entitled to have and retain keys for all the doors to the Property but shall not be entitled to use these to enter the Property without the consent of the Tenant (save in an emergency).

6.3 Any notices or other documents shall be deemed served on the Tenant during the tenancy by either being left at the Property or by being sent to the Tenant at the Property by first-class post. Notices shall be deemed served the day after being left at the property or the day after posting.

6.4 Any person other than the Tenant who pays all or part of the rent due under this Agreement to the Landlord shall be deemed to have made such payment as agent for and on behalf of the Tenant which the Landlord shall be entitled to assume without enquiry.

6.5 Any personal items left behind at the end of the tenancy after the Tenant has vacated (which the Tenant has not removed in accordance with clause 1.13 of this Agreement) shall be considered abandoned if they have not been removed within 14 days of written notice to the Tenant from the Landlord or if the Landlord has been unable to trace the Tenant by taking reasonable steps to do so. After this period the Landlord may remove or dispose of the items as he thinks fit. The Tenant shall be liable for the reasonable disposal costs which may be deducted from the proceeds of sale (if any), and the Tenant shall remain liable for any balance. Any net proceeds of sale to be returned to the Tenant at the forwarding address provided to the Landlord.

6.6 In the event of damage to or destruction of the Property by any of the risks insured against by the Landlord the Tenant shall be relieved from payment of the Rent to the extent that the Tenant's use and enjoyment of the Property is thereby prevented and from performance of his obligations as to the state and condition of the Property to the extent of and so long as there prevails such damage or destruction (except to the extent that the insurance is prejudiced by any act or default of the Tenant).

6.7 Where the context so admits:

6.7.1 The 'Landlord' includes the persons from time to time entitled to receive the Rent.

6.7.2 The 'Tenant' includes any persons deriving title under the Tenant.

6.7.3 The 'Property' includes any part or parts of the Property and all of the Landlord's fixtures and fittings at or upon the Property.

6.7.4 All references to the singular shall include the plural and vice versa and any obligations or liabilities of more than one person shall be joint and several (this means that they will each be liable for all sums due under this Agreement, not just liable for a proportionate part) and an obligation on the part of a party shall include an obligation not to allow or permit the breach of that obligation.

6.7.5 All references to 'he', 'him' and 'his' shall be taken to include 'she', 'her' and 'hers'.

Additional
provisions (if any)
....
....
....
....
....
....
....
....
....
....
....
....
....

Signed and executed as a Deed by the following parties:

Landlord	Tenant	Guarantor*
....	....	....
....	....	....
Landlord(s)' name(s)	Tenant(s)' name(s)	Guarantor's name
....	....	....
....	....	....
Landlord(s)' signature(s)	Tenant(s)' signature(s)	Guarantor's signature

In the presence of:

Witness signature	Witness signature	Witness signature ....
Full name	Full name	Full name ....
Address	Address	Address ....

*Delete as applicable.

4

Fig 7.1 Example Assured Shorthold Tenancy Agreement

- **Duration:** An AST can be for any length of time. I would always suggest a tenancy of six months as the tenant has the right to run the duration of the tenancy unless there is a breach on either party. See below.

- **Running expenses:** It sets out who is liable for the running expenses of the property.

- **Tenant obligations:** It details the tenant's obligations to the property and the landlord, such as maintenance, or informing the landlord of problems in good time or reporting damage.

- **Landlord obligations:** It details the landlord's obligations to the property and the tenant, such as privacy and timeliness of repairs. Under sections 11 to 16 of the Landlord and Tenant Act 1985, a landlord is obliged to keep in repair the structure and exterior of the house; the water, electricity and gas supplies; and the heating. If the tenanted property forms part of a larger building (e.g. a block of flats) which the landlord owns or controls, the landlord will also be responsible for the repair of the common parts and installations.

Both the tenant and the landlord have to sign, with both signatures, witnessed by an independent third party.

An AST must be compliant with the Unfair Terms in Consumer Contracts Regulations 1999, otherwise it will be deemed invalid. The Office of Fair Trading (OFT) has issued a document called 'Guidance on Unfair Terms in Tenancy Agreements'. This can be bought from the OFT or downloaded for free from its website at www.oft.gov.uk. This directive protects tenants from any clauses which exclude or limit their rights. For example, the introduction of penalty clauses which don't reflect genuine cost to the landlord or general costs which are not specified.

Ready-drafted ASTs are available from Lawpack, and an example is provided on pages 80 to 83; visit www.lawpack.co.uk for details. Landlords can obtain further information about their legal rights and obligations with Lawpack's Residential Lettings guide, written by specialist solicitor Tessa Shepperson.

An eviction order

To commence the legal process of evicting a tenant, the landlord must have a 'ground' for eviction and serve the proper notice on the tenant before any court action is started.

There are two categories for grounds of possession: mandatory and discretionary. It's advisable only to evict on mandatory grounds as the judge will have no option but to grant an order for possession. With regard to discretionary grounds, the tenant can defend the claim by possibly obtaining Legal Aid, which could end up being costly for you should you lose.

Here are the two most common mandatory grounds for possession. If the tenancy is an AST, the landlord can serve a Housing Act 1988 section 21 notice after the fixed term has expired. Alternatively, if the tenant is in rent arrears of eight weeks/two months, both at the time of the service of the notice (a section 8 notice) and the court hearing, ground 8 in schedule 2 of the Housing Act 1988 can be used.

It's recommended that you hand the notices to the tenant personally. Do make sure that your paperwork is completely accurate, as judges are wary of granting possession orders and will refuse to do so on the grounds of mistakes.

At no time can a landlord evict a tenant in any way other than through the courts. To manhandle him out of the property is a criminal offence.

To be honest, eviction is an extremely complicated process. As a result, we advise you always to consult a solicitor, but if you do want to find out more about the subject, then do read Lawpack's *Residential Lettings* guide or speak to your Citizens Advice Bureau. If you do decide to act on your own behalf, the Court Service do publish a series of leaflets, which are available at County Courts or online at www.hmcourts-service.gov.uk.

We have to face reality, though. The procedure is stressful and will take a long time. It can potentially involve you losing six months' rent and will include court and solicitor's fees plus the threat of damage to your property.

To avoid such a battle, you could offer to pay your tenant to leave. This option could be cheaper. I would suggest one month's rent being fair. This will pay the deposit for their next property.

Try to initiate a friendly separation. Don't add fuel to an already fiery situation by losing your temper and threatening immediate court action.

Statistically only three per cent of tenants tend to be bad tenants – bad tenants being tenants who have no intention of paying the rent, not tenants who lose their job and can't pay their rent. If a tenant loses his job, it's more than likely that he is going to get another job. If he has been a relatively good payer of the rent, be patient with him.

In my experience, I would say that the three per cent statistic is right. The majority of people wish to settle in a home and feel secure. The best way for them to feel secure is for them to pay their rent on time.

Insurers

You'll have to enter legal contracts with insurance companies to cover you against certain risks. Your insurance will only ever be valid if you've originally told the truth on your proposal form when obtaining the insurance. The main insurances you'll take out when investing in property will be:

- **Buildings insurance:** The insurance you pay to cover the property against fire, vandalism, water damage or weather damage.

- **Contents insurance:** This is insurance for items such as carpets, furniture and other fittings that you've provided for the property.

- **Rental guarantee:** This is insurance against your tenant defaulting on the rental payments.

- **Emergency assistance:** This insurance will cover the costs of any emergency repairs that have to be carried out, including all call-out charges.

When filling out the form the insurance company will ask you about any previous claims. If you've got some, then reveal them. If you do have to make a claim and you haven't told the company about a previous claim, it doesn't have to pay out. It's very easy for it to find out if you've had a claim as it has a central register of all claims paid out.

If you do lie and it catches you out, you'll find it difficult to get insurance in the future, as you may be put on a blacklist which is accessible to all insurers.

Don't rely on general household insurance for a residential property and do make sure that the insurance company knows that your property is rented. There are certain policies which do exclude asylum seekers, housing benefit claimants or students as tenants, so check each clause carefully.

Letting agents

If you do decide to use a letting agent, then you have to read his terms and conditions very carefully. Watch for:

- **Timeliness of payment:** Check to see how soon the letting agent has to hand over the money, once the tenant has provided it. I wouldn't accept any period longer than three days.

- **Get-out clauses:** If you decide not to use the letting agent any more, check to see how easy it is to get out. One agent tried to sue me for all the lost commission he would have earned, even though I was now collecting the rent! If you want to use a letting agent at first and then take over in six months, inform the letting agent of this intention. You may be able to strike a deal where you have a realistically priced option to get out of the contract.

Regulatory

There are five main regulations governing the renting of properties:

1. Gas safety
2. Electrical safety
3. Fire resistance
4. Tenancy deposit schemes
5. Property licensing for houses in multiple occupation

Gas safety

If there is gas at the property, then you have to get a landlord's safety record from a CORGI (Council for Registered Gas Installers)-registered engineer. He will inspect the:

- Central heating boiler
- Oven and hob
- Gas fire
- Gas meters

The property needs to be inspected annually and a copy of the certificate needs to be presented to the tenant at the start of the tenancy and each year thereafter.

If you don't get one of these certificates and someone suffers or even dies from carbon monoxide poisoning, you could face a hefty fine and imprisonment. The guilt will be even worse.

For further advice, contact the Health and Safety Executive, which produces the Health & Safety Executive Code of Practice and Guidance. The obligations of landlords are summarised in the leaflet 'Landlords: A Guide to Landlords' Duties', available free. Also, go online at www.hse.gov.uk.

Electrical safety

A yearly inspection is needed for all electrical appliances supplied with the property by an NICEIC (National Inspection Council for Electrical Installation Contracting) contractor. Basically, anything electrical will need to be examined and passed by the NICEIC contractor.

So it's quite obvious – keep the number of electrical items to a minimum! The fewer electrical items you supply, the less there is likely to go wrong. You don't need your tenant ringing you up at 6am complaining about the kettle not working.

There is no NICEIC certificate issued, but an inspection will cover you from being sued if any electrical appliance were to harm your tenants or their guests.

Electrical items also must comply with the Plugs and Sockets Safety Regulations. This shouldn't be an issue if the appliances were purchased recently.

Fire resistance

All upholstered furniture must comply with the Furniture and Furnishings (Fire Safety) Regulations 1988. You can tell if the furniture is compliant because there will be a label in the cushioning. Any furniture purchased after 1990 will automatically comply with all fire regulations.

Although it's not a legal requirement, I would recommend that smoke alarms be installed in rented properties to cover you against any negligence claim if you were to be sued.

Tenancy deposit schemes

Since 6 April 2007, all landlords must adhere to the new laws surrounding tenants' deposits for ASTs created in the UK.

The legislation has come about to ensure the following:

- The tenant gets back all or part of his deposit to which he is entitled to.

- It's now easier to resolve disputes between landlords and tenants regarding the return of deposits.

- Any landlord who acts unfairly is punished financially.

There are two types of tenancy deposit schemes available for landlords:

1. Insurance-based schemes
2. Custodial schemes

Insurance-based schemes

As it sounds, you receive the deposit and then pay an insurance premium to cover the costs if you and the tenant were to get into a dispute. My deposits are held under this scheme and I pay a £30 one-off payment per deposit.

When the tenant pays you the deposit, by law you must provide information to the tenant on how his deposit is protected within 14 days. The prescribed information includes:

- The contact details of the tenancy deposit scheme selected
- Your contact details
- How the tenant can apply for the release of his deposit
- Information explaining the purpose of the tenant's deposit
- What to do if there is a dispute about the deposit

There is no official legal document which you have to use to provide the tenant with this information, but Lawpack has produced a *Tenancy Deposit Protection Form* (available at www.lawpack.co.uk) which includes all the information you need and it saves you all the hassle of writing one yourself.

It's important that you give your tenant the right information; otherwise you may find that you're unable to seek possession from the tenant and you may be liable to pay him a sum of money equal to three times the amount of the deposit.

When the tenancy ends you agree with the tenant how much is to be returned and you return this amount on a date agreed by you both.

If there is a dispute, then this disputed amount needs to be transferred to the scheme, the remainder returned to the tenant and then the scheme resolves the dispute based on the evidence of both parties.

Custodial schemes

Again, as it sounds, the scheme keeps custody of the deposit, so when you receive the tenant's deposit you pay over the deposit to the scheme. The interest earned from this money is set aside to pay for the running of the scheme.

When the tenant pays you the deposit you have to inform the tenant on how his deposit is protected within 14 days. Again, you're legally obliged to give your tenant the same prescribed information as for the insurance-based scheme (see above). Lawpack's *Tenancy Deposit Protection Form* can help you with this.

When the tenancy ends you agree with the tenant how the deposit should be divided and if you're in agreement, the scheme returns the agreed amounts.

If there is a dispute, the deposit is held by the scheme until the dispute is resolved, usually by the courts. Once it's resolved the scheme returns the amounts agreed by the courts or whatever medium they used to resolve the dispute.

Resolving disputes

The most cost effective way to resolve a dispute is outside of the courts. A free service is offered and if both you and the tenant agree, the dispute can be resolved by the Alternative Dispute Resolution (ADR) service. If such an option is chosen, both of you agree to be bound by the ADR's decision. I suggest that if the dispute is for more than £1,000, you go through the courts as they will be better equipped to understand all the evidence. Otherwise, opt for the ADR.

The three scheme providers

There are three scheme providers available to landlords – one custodial and two insurance-backed schemes.

Type	Name	About
Custodial	The Deposit Protection Service (DPS)	The DPS, the only custodial deposit protection scheme, is free to use and open to all landlords and letting agents. For more information, call 0870 707 1 707.
Insurance	Tenancy Deposit Solutions Ltd (TDSL)	TDSL is a partnership between the National Landlords Association and Hamilton Fraser Insurance. For more information, call 0871 703 0552.

Insurance	The Tenancy Deposit Scheme (TDS)	TDS is an insurance-backed deposit protection and dispute resolution scheme run by The Dispute Service that builds on a scheme established in 2003 to provide dispute resolution and complaints handling for the lettings industry. For more information, call 0845 226 7837.

What happens if you don't use a tenancy deposit scheme

The tenant can apply to the local County Court and order you to either repay the deposit back to the tenant or force you to protect it in a scheme. If you don't, then you can be forced to pay an amount of up to three times the deposit amount to the tenant. You have been warned!

Property licensing for houses in multiple occupation

A house in multiple occupation (HMO) is a property, or part of a property (such as a flat), which has more than one household that shares an amenity, such as a bathroom, toilet or kitchen. A household is defined as either a single person, a couple, or a couple with children and other members of their family.

So a flat with the owner and a lodger living there would be deemed as an HMO, as well as a 15-roomed house full of students or asylum seekers!

Now, there are two forms of licensing:

1. Mandatory licensing
2. Additional licensing

Mandatory licensing

Mandatory licensing means just that. You **must** get a property licence if you own a HMO (as defined above) and your HMO meets all of these conditions:

1. The building has three or more storeys

2. There are five or more people living in the building

Basements and attics are included in the count of storeys. Also, if you only occupy two storeys of a three-storey building (such as a two-storey apartment above a shop), your HMO is part of a three-storey building so it will fall under the need for mandatory licensing if there are five or more people in the HMO.

Failure to get a licence can result in a £20,000 fine, six months' imprisonment and a clawback of all the rent you've received while you've been operating without a licence.

To obtain a licence you, or the most suitable person considered holding the licence (such as a property manager of the HMO), must make an application to the council. The fee varies from council to council and lasts for five years.

Additional licensing

Councils have the power to enforce landlords to get an additional licence for HMO properties falling outside of the three-storey/five-tenant rule for mandatory licensing.

This is for areas where individual councils have an ongoing problem with poorly run bedsits in not so desirable areas where there are risks to the actual occupants or to the public outside.

I think we all know the streets and areas where it's bedsit heaven and living conditions are poor, or there is plenty of antisocial behaviour. This additional licensing gives the council powers to either close down these HMOs or force landlords to improve standards.

To find out if a HMO is subject to additional licensing, you need to contact the council direct. My experience is that most councils have held off introducing additional licensing. It may be because councils are getting used to mandatory licensing and they may introduce additional licensing at a later date.

All-encompassing

You'll also be legally bound by the normal all-encompassing laws of the land which apply to us all. These include:

1. The law of tort – negligence and personal injury

2. Criminal law

The law of tort

Even though you may have all the safety records in place, you still owe a duty of care to your tenant and anyone who enters your property. If it can be shown that you were negligent in any way, you could be sued and ordered to pay damages.

As a landlord, you're liable for any damages if the following apply:

1. your tenant or anyone entering your investment property suffers an injury; and

2. you owed a duty of care to the person entering your investment property who suffered the personal injury; and

3. you breached that duty of care.

So, for example, if Zak, the landlord, failed to fix the cooker socket in the kitchen and the tenant's guest, Liz, suffered an electric shock burn, then Zak would be liable to compensate Liz for her injury.

This is because:

1. Liz suffered injury;

2. Zak owed a duty of care, as it's realistically expected that a tenant would invite a guest into their property; and

3. Zak breached that duty of care, as he had not fixed the socket when asked to by the tenant.

Criminal law

Even if your tenant hasn't paid you any rent for two months, you cannot 'send the boys round'. Threatening your tenant or being violent to your tenant because he hasn't paid you any rent is no justification for your behaviour in the eyes of the law.

Harassment legislation entitles the tenant to bring civil proceedings himself against you for an injunction and/or damages. Alternatively, the tenant can complain to the local authorities, who may proceed with criminal prosecution, which may end up in a fine or two years' imprisonment if you're found guilty.

Examples of action which are seen as harassment are threats of/actual violence, disconnection of the gas and electricity, and entering the property without the consent of the tenant.

Should you be accused of harassment, stop visiting or contacting the tenant by telephone. Consider approaching him through a solicitor and always contact him in writing. Signed and dated copies of correspondence should be kept at all times.

In the end, remember, it's only money! This is the phrase I say to myself when I get stressed when a tenant 'does a runner' and leaves me with £1,500 owing. As I said in the Introduction, you have to be a responsible person and realise that if you want to take investing in property seriously, you have to act lawfully in every way.

CHAPTER 8

Reference chapter

In this chapter you'll find all the addresses, phone numbers and websites you'll need to get started in property investment. This chapter covers:

1. 100 per cent LTV mortgage providers*

2. Buy-to-let mortgage providers*

(*Information reproduced by kind permission of Moneynet and correct at the time of publication. Check www.moneynet.co.uk for the most up-to-date figures.)

3. List of property websites

4. Mortgage brokers

5. List of accommodation projects

6. List of hotspots

7. List of freephone/lo-call providers

8. List of credit-checking agencies

9. Guaranteed rent and maintenance providers

10. Letting agents

11. Management software providers

12. Local newspapers

13. List of auctioneers

100 per cent LTV mortgage providers

100 per cent mortgage providers can fund the whole purchase price of a property. Some providers below also refund the valuation and legal fees. Some offer in excess of 100 per cent. They also offer up to five times your salary plus your partner's salary as total borrowings. These lenders are giving it to you on a plate! Read the notes on each lender to find out how much they lend.

To obtain the following figures, I based the amount of mortgage required as £100,000 and the salary to be £50,000. The total costs are based on the number of years the mortgage is kept, i.e. in this instance I used the average figure of seven years.

Lender:	Yorkshire Building Society
Rate:	0% – six months, then 5.69% – 31/05/2011. Then variable rate (6.40% currently)
APR:	6.4%
Product type:	Stepped fixed
Mortgage type:	Repayment
Total cost (for seven years):	£49,609.12

Monthly costs	
Initial monthly payment:	Nil
Interest payment at lender's Standard Variable Rate:	£668.27

Set-up costs	
Higher lending charge:	N/A
Arrangement fee:	£395
Less cashback:	£400
Net costs:	£0–5
Other incentives:	None

Conditions

Early redemption penalty:	5% of amount repaid until 31/05/2009, then 4% and 3% until 31/05/2011
Conditional insurances:	None

How much can you borrow

Single income:	3.5 times
Joint incomes:	3.5 x main income plus 3.5 x second income or 0 x joint income

Additional features

- The scheme is 0% fixed for the first six months and then 5.69% fixed until 31/05/2011.
- The ability to overpay, underpay and take payment holidays.
- The lender charges interest on a daily basis.
- Enhanced income multiples are available for purchase for those aged over 40 – refer to lender for details.
- Free mortgage payment protection insurance for the first six months.
- The lender's acceptance is based upon affordability. The income multiples shown above are for guidance only.
- Capital repayments up to 10% are allowed each year without penalty.

Lender:	Yorkshire Building Society
Rate:	0% – six months, then 5.50% – six months, then 5.75% – four years. Then variable rate (6.40% currently)
APR:	6.4%
Product type:	Stepped tracker
Mortgage type:	Repayment
Total cost (for seven years):	£49,871.23

Monthly costs

Initial monthly payment:	Nil
Interest payment at lender's Standard Variable Rate:	£668.27

Set-up costs

Higher lending charge:	N/A
Arrangement fee:	£395
Less cashback:	£400
Net costs:	£0–5
Other incentives:	None

Conditions

Early redemption penalty:	5% of amount repaid within three years, then 4% and 3% until year five
Conditional insurances:	None

How much can you borrow

Single income:	3.5 times
Joint incomes:	3.5 x main income plus 3.5 x second income or 0 x joint income

Additional features

- The scheme is 0% for the first six months, then the Bank of England Base Rate (currently 4.50%) plus 1.00% for six months, and then plus 1.25% for the next four years.

- The ability to overpay, underpay and take payment holidays. The lender charges interest on a daily basis.

- Enhanced income multiples are available for purchase for those aged over 40 – refer to lender for details.

- Free mortgage payment protection insurance for the first six months. The lender's acceptance is based upon affordability. The income multiples shown above are for guidance only.

- Capital repayments up to 10% are allowed each year without penalty.

Lender:	Scottish Widows Bank
Rate:	4.94% – one year, then 5.44% – one year, then 5.69% – one year. Then variable rate (5.94% currently)
APR:	5.9%
Product type:	Stepped discount
Mortgage type:	Repayment
Total cost (for seven years):	£52,502.38

Monthly costs

Initial monthly payment:	£580.51
Interest payment at lender's Standard Variable Rate:	£639.97

Set-up costs

Higher lending charge:	N/A
Arrangement fee:	Nil
Less cashback:	Nil
Net costs:	Nil
Other incentives:	Valuation fees refunded – maximum of £250. Legal fees refunded – maximum of £150

Conditions

Early redemption penalty:	2% of advance within three years on full redemption
Conditional insurances:	None

How much can you borrow

Single income:	4 times

Joint incomes:	4 x main income plus 1 x second income or 3 x joint income

Additional features

- Not available in Northern Ireland.
- Available only to medical doctors, dentists, solicitors, accountants, vets and teachers (must be fully qualified and practising.)
- The lender charges interest on a daily basis.
- The scheme is 1.00% discount for the first year, 0.50% discount for the second year and then 0.25% in the third year.
- Available with or without an offset mortgage facility. The mortgage deposit account must be opened in the same name(s) as the mortgage account.
- The valuation fee is refunded on completion.
- Professional mortgage: Lending available up to 110% LTV. Additional 10% is on an unsecured basis over a maximum 10-year period.
- At any time you can apply for a payment holiday or reduced monthly payments for up to 12 months. To take advantage of this, you must have a Mortgage Reserve Account in place.

Lender:	**Royal Bank of Scotland**
Rate:	5.14% – 01/04/2008. Then variable rate (6.59% currently)
APR:	6.8%
Product type:	Discount
Mortgage type:	Repayment
Total cost (for seven years):	£57,816.37

Monthly costs

Initial monthly payment:	£592.17
Interest payment at lender's Standard Variable Rate:	£680.13

Set-up costs

Higher lending charge:	£3,000
Arrangement fee:	Nil
Less cashback:	Nil
Net costs:	£3,000
Other incentives:	None

Conditions

Early redemption penalty:	2% of sum repaid until 01/04/2007, then 1% until 01/04/2008
Conditional insurances:	None

How much can you borrow

Single income:	3.25 times
Joint incomes:	3.25 x main income plus 1 x second income or 2.75 x joint income

Additional features

- Available for royalties account holders only.
- 1.45% discount. The lender charges interest on a daily basis.
- Free accident, sickness and unemployment cover available for three months.
- Higher income multiples available for professionals.
- For customer borrowing 100% LTV and borrowing £120,000 or more, it can add up to £3,000 of non-bank fees (£1,000 for loans below £120,000).

Lender:	Portman
Rate:	5.25% – 31/03/2011. Then variable rate (6.50% currently)
APR:	6.3%
Product type:	Fixed

Mortgage type:	Repayment
Total cost (for seven years):	£52,954.94

Monthly costs

Initial monthly payment:	£606.17
Interest payment at lender's Standard Variable Rate:	£683.18

Set-up costs

Higher lending charge:	N/A
Arrangement fee:	£299
Less cashback:	Nil
Net costs:	£299
Other incentives:	Valuation fees refunded

Conditions

Early redemption penalty:	5% of the balance until 31/03/2011, plus fee of £175
Conditional insurances:	None

How much can you borrow

Single income:	4 times
Joint incomes:	4 x main income plus 1 x second income or 3 x joint income

Additional features

- Not available in Northern Ireland.
- Capital repayments up to 5% allowed each 12-month period until 31/03/2008. The minimum age is 21 (if the mortgage is in joint names, both applicants must be 21).
- The first applicant's minimum salary must be £20,000.
- The fee shown is a booking fee and it's non-refundable.

- Available on a repayment basis only.
- No shared ownership or right to buys.

Lender:	Scottish Widows Bank
Rate:	5.29% – 31/03/2008. Then variable rate (5.94% currently)
APR:	6.0%
Product type:	Fixed
Mortgage type:	Repayment
Total cost (for seven years):	£53,053.85

Monthly costs

Initial monthly payment:	£600.99
Interest payment at lender's Standard Variable Rate:	£639.97

Set-up costs

Higher lending charge:	N/A
Arrangement fee:	£295
Less cashback:	Nil
Net costs:	£295
Other incentives:	Valuation fees refunded – maximum of £250. Legal fees refunded – maximum of £150

Conditions

Early redemption penalty:	3% of sum repaid until 31/03/2008
Conditional insurances:	None

How much can you borrow

Single income:	4 times

Joint incomes:	4 x main income plus 1 x second income or 3 x joint income

Additional features

- Not available in Northern Ireland.
- Chequebook facility available.
- Available only to doctors, dentists, accountants, solicitors, teachers and vets.
- The lender charges interest on a daily basis.
- At any time you can apply for a payment holiday or reduced monthly payments for up to 12 months. To take advantage of this, you must have a Mortgage Reserve Account in place.
- Professional mortgage: Lending available up to 110% LTV. The additional 10% is on an unsecured basis over a maximum ten-year period. The valuation fee is refunded on completion.
- The arrangement fee shown is a non-refundable booking fee.
- Capital repayments up to 10% are allowed each year without penalty (a minimum of £1,000).

Lender:	Nat West
Rate:	5.55% – 30/04/2008. Then variable rate (6.59% currently)
APR:	7.0%
Product type:	Fixed
Mortgage type:	Repayment
Total cost (for seven years):	£56,144.08

Monthly costs

Initial monthly payment:	£616.44
Interest payment at lender's Standard Variable Rate:	£680.13

Set-up costs

Higher lending charge:	£515
Arrangement fee:	£195
Less cashback:	Nil
Net costs:	£710
Other incentives:	Valuation fees refunded

Conditions

Early redemption penalty:	2% of sum repaid until 30/04/2007, then 1% until 30/04/2008
Conditional insurances:	None

How much can you borrow

Single income:	4.25 times
Joint incomes:	4.25 x main income plus 1 x second income or 3.1 x joint income

Additional features

- Not available in Northern Ireland.

- No valuation fee.

- The interest is calculated daily.

- Increased income multiples for professionals (maximum loan of £250,000) of up to five x professional salary plus one x second salary, or up to 2.75 x joint salary for joint applications.

- Applicants must be fully qualified members of one of the following professions: medical doctors, pharmacists, opticians, dentists, vets, solicitors and accountants (minimum salary – £20,000, minimum age – 23, and they must meet all standard affordability guidelines).

- The lender's acceptance is based upon affordability. The income multiples shown above are for guidance only. Capital repayments up to 10% are allowed each year without penalty.

- Legal/survey fees can be added to the loan subject to the maximum LTV (in the case of 100% LTV mortgages, a maximum of £1,000 can be added over 100% LTV for loans below £120,000; a maximum of £3,000 can be added for loans of £120,000 and above).

Buy-to-let mortgage providers

If you wish to approach a lender direct, then you can refer to this list. The mortgage companies listed below will fund anywhere between 50 and 90 per cent of the purchase price of an investment residential property. Some of these lenders require that you're employed or earning in excess of a certain limit. I've listed them in descending LTVs. Thus the higher up the list your choice of lender is, the greater the buying power you have.

90 per cent LTV

Lender:	Capital Home Loans
Rate:	4.99% until 31/07/2009
APR:	7.4%
Interest charged:	Annually
Product type:	Fixed
Early redemption penalty:	6% of redeeming balance until 31/07/2011
Repayment method:	Interest only
Life insurance required:	No
Acceptable areas:	Mainland England, Wales and Northern Ireland

Additional features

- The minimum valuation of any property is £40,000 (with a minimum of £50,000 for one-bedroom flats/maisonettes).
- The minimum lease allowed is 35 years on the maturity of the mortgage.
- The completion fee is 1.25% of advance (a minimum of £300).

- Applicants must be residents and paying UK tax for a minimum of three years.

- Applicants must be existing homeowners with an outstanding mortgage or be limited companies/property developers/commercial landlords.

- Rental income must be at least 115% of the actual interest rate.

- No ex-local authority flats/maisonettes or studio flats (refer to lender for exceptions). No DSS tenants, diplomatic immunity or specific trusts.

- The scheme is fixed until 31/07/2009, then the Bank of England Base Rate (currently 5.75%) plus 1.75% for the term.

- An Assured Shorthold Tenancy Agreement or company letting agreement is required.

- CCJs are considered – a maximum of two CCJs to a combined value of £500 and they must be satisfied for at least two years.

Lender:	Astra Mortgages
Rate:	6.23% for five years
APR:	6.8%
Interest charged:	Daily
Product type:	Fixed
Early redemption penalty:	5%, 5%, 5%, 4%, then 3% within five years of outstanding balance
Repayment method:	Interest only
Life insurance required:	No
Acceptable areas:	England and Wales

Additional features

- Introduced business only.

- The lender is Norwich and Peterborough Building Society.

- No property developers, self-certifications, DSS tenants, ex-pats, foreign nationals, asylum seekers or diplomatic immunity applications.

- The minimum age is 18 for the main income earner (with the minimum of a £25,000 income).
- Freehold and leasehold (with 50 years' left at the end of the mortgage term).
- An assured shorthold tenancy of six to 12 months is required. The property must not be let to immediate family members.
- Company lets are acceptable over one to five years. Longer lets are acceptable subject to no more than five years remaining on the letting agreement.
- New-build flats (under one-year old – maximum LTV 80%).
- A maximum of four storeys on ex-local authority developments.
- Total blocks of flats are accepted, provided that the landlord owns the freehold. The unit restriction in the block – eight maximum in unit.
- No freehold flats/maisonettes.
- No pre-fabricated properties, Ministry of Defence, housing association houses or flats.
- A maximum advance of £2m per property and £5m per borrower.
- Rental coverage – 115%.
- The scheme is fixed for five years, then the Bank of England Base Rate (currently 5.75%) plus 0.95% for the term.

Lender:	Bristol & West
Rate:	6.29% until 31/08/2012
APR:	7.6%
Interest charged:	Annually
Product type:	Fixed
Early redemption penalty:	5% interest until 31/08/2012
Repayment method:	Interest only
Life insurance required:	No
Acceptable areas:	England, Scotland and Wales

Additional features

- The scheme is fixed until 31/08/2012, then the Bank of England Base Rate (currently 5.75%) plus 1.75%.
- The minimum valuation of any property is £40,000.
- DSS tenants, students (multiple tenancies (not houses in multiple occupation (HMOs)), maximum of four) allowed. No holiday lets or family members are allowed.
- No first-time buyers.
- Rental income yield calculated at 100% of pay rate.
- The minimum income of £15,000 is required.
- A maximum of 15 properties per applicant is allowed. The total borrowing is £2.5m.
- Borrowers must be over 21.
- Employed applicants must show their last month's payslips and employer's references.
- Self-employed applicants must show agreed tax assessments from the latest year and the latest year's audited accounts (prepared by a chartered, certified or authorised public accountant). A letter from a chartered, certified or authorised public accountant confirming the applicant's salary or share of profit.
- A minimum loan for remortgage is £25,001.
- Capital repayments up to 10% are allowed each year without penalty.
- Excludes properties located in office blocks and local authority office conversions for ALL product types. Flats in converted office blocks and speculatively converted ex-local authority blocks are unacceptable.

Lender:	Bank of Ireland
Rate:	6.39% until 30/09/2012
APR:	7.3%
Interest charged:	Annually
Product type:	Fixed
Early redemption penalty:	5% of the amount repaid until 30/09/2012

Repayment method:	Interest only
Life insurance required:	No
Acceptable areas:	England, Wales and Northern Ireland

Additional features

- Available for remortgages only.
- Call lender to discuss the minimum lease allowed.
- Letting to family members, multiple occupancies, DSS tenants, council or student tenants isn't allowed.
- Rental income yield calculated at 100% of pay rate.
- A maximum of four properties per applicant (after reaching four properties applicants are assessed against professional criteria). The total borrowing is £2.5m.
- Borrowers must be over 21.
- The scheme is fixed until 30/09/2012, then the Bank of England Base Rate (currently 5.75%) plus 1.75%.
- The minimum valuation of any property is £40,000.
- The legal fees are paid if the lender's solicitor is used.
- A free valuation is available, up to a maximum property value of £500,000, when the lender instructs the valuation.
- A lending fee of £195 must be paid on completion or at the final repayment.
- Also available to professional landlords (they must be aged over 25).
- Professional landlords, who have five or more properties in their portfolios.
- Professional landlords – no limit to the number of properties – maximum portfolio limit of £20m.
- Professional landlords – rental yield 125% of pay rate.
- Professional landlords can use surplus earned income to make up rental shortfalls.
- Professional landlords – a minimum loan of £50,000.

85 per cent LTV

Lender:	Paragon
Rate:	4.49% until 31/01/2010
APR:	8.2%
Interest charged:	Annually
Product type:	Fixed
Arrangement fee:	£4,250
Early redemption penalty:	4% interest until 31/12/2012 or four years, whichever is longer, and £150 plus any product-related charges
Repayment method:	Interest only
Life insurance required:	No
Acceptable areas:	England, Wales and Scotland

Monthly costs

Initial monthly payment:	£319

Additional features

- The minimum valuation of any property is £50,000.
- The minimum lease allowed is 40 years on the maturity of the mortgage.
- No ex -local authority, freehold flats or maisonettes, or shared ownership properties are allowed.
- The lender will lend to limited companies.
- The lender may consider a single property divided into a maximum of 20 units. The minimum valuation is £100,000.
- The lender may consider a single property divided into a maximum of 10 units. The minimum valuation is £75,000.
- The minimum age of applicants is 21.
- A maximum aggregate loan up to to £20m may be advanced to an applicant on a property portfolio.

- The scheme is fixed until 31/01/2010, then three-month Libor (currently 6.40%) plus 1.50% for the term.
- Where Paragon assesses an application based purely on the gross rental income from the property, the rent must equal or exceed 125% of the interest-only payment calculated currently at 5.75%.
- An assured shorthold tenancy subject to a minimum of six months and a maximum of 12 months.

Lender:	Capital Home Loans
Rate:	4.99% until 31/07/2009
APR:	7.4%
Interest charged:	Annually
Product type:	Fixed
Arrangement fee:	£1,062.50
Early redemption penalty:	6% of redeeming balance until 31/07/2011
Repayment method:	Interest only
Life insurance required:	No
Acceptable areas:	Mainland England, Wales and Northern Ireland

Monthly costs

Initial monthly payment:	£354

Additional features

- The minimum valuation of any property is £40,000 (with a minimum of £50,000 for one-bedroom flats/maisonettes).
- The minimum lease allowed is 35 years on the maturity of the mortgage.
- The completion fee is 1.25% of the advance (a minimum of £300).
- Applicants must be residents and paying UK tax for a minimum of three years.

- Applicants must be existing homeowners with an outstanding mortgage or be limited companies/property developers/commercial landlords.
- Rental income must be at least 115% of the actual interest rate.
- No ex -local authority flats/maisonettes or studio flats (refer to lender for exceptions). No DSS tenants, diplomatic immunity or specific trusts.
- The scheme is fixed until 31/07/2009, then the Bank of England Base Rate (currently 5.75%) plus 1.75% for the term.
- An Assured Shorthold Tenancy Agreement or company letting agreement is required.
- CCJs are considered. A maximum of two CCJs to a combined value of £500. They must be satisfied for at least two years.

Lender:	Norwich & Peterborough
Rate:	5.13% for two years
APR:	7.5%
Interest charged:	Daily
Product type:	Discount
Arrangement fee:	£425
Early redemption penalty:	5% of outstanding balance within three years, then 4% and 3% within the next two years
Repayment method:	Interest only
Life insurance required:	No
Acceptable areas:	England and Wales

Monthly costs

Initial monthly payment:	£364

Additional features

- No property developers, self-certifications, DSS tenants, ex-pats, foreign nationals, asylum seekers or diplomatic immunity applications.

- The minimum age is 18 for the main income earner (with the minimum of a £25,000 income).
- Freehold and leasehold (with 50 years left at the end of the mortgage term).
- An assured shorthold tenancy of six to 12 months. The property must not be let to immediate family members.
- Company lets are acceptable over one to five years. Longer lets are acceptable subject to no more than five years remaining on the letting agreement.
- New-build flats – maximum LTV is 80%.
- A maximum of four storeys on ex-local authority developments.
- Total blocks of flats are accepted, provided that the landlord owns the freehold. The unit restriction in the block – eight maximum in unit.
- No freehold flats/maisonettes.
- No pre-fabricated properties, Ministry of Defence, or housing association houses or flats.
- Maximum advance – £2,000,000 per property, £5,000,000 per borrower.
- Rental coverage – 125%.
- Discount – 2.61% (Buy-to-Let Standard Variable Rate – 7.74%).
- The minimum valuation of any property outside the branch is £75,000.

Lender:	Dunfermline Building Society
Rate:	5.14% until 31/01/2010
APR:	7.9%
Interest charged:	Annually
Product type:	Fixed
Arrangement fee:	£1,999
Early redemption penalty:	4% of capital repaid until 31/01/2010, plus £199

Repayment method:	Interest only
Life insurance required:	No
Acceptable areas:	England, Wales and Scotland

Monthly costs

Initial monthly payment:	£365

Additional features

- The minimum valuation of any property is £50,000.
- The minimum lease allowed is 30 years on the maturity of the mortgage.
- DSS tenants, council or student tenants are not allowed.
- The lender has no set criteria. It will accept/decline each application on its own merits.
- The maximum term is 20 years.
- A maximum portfolio of five buy-to-let properties with the lender, up to a maximum value of £1m.
- The maximum advance is negotiable.
- Rental cover must be at least 125% of the loan repayments. The Bank of England Base Rate (currently 5.75%) plus 1.00%.
- Capital repayments up to 10% are allowed each year without penalty.
- The maximum portfolio size is £1m.
- Buy-to-Let Standard Variable Rate – 7.74%.

Lender:	**West Bromwich Building Society**
Rate:	5.19% until 30/11/2009
APR:	7.5%
Interest charged:	Daily
Product type:	Fixed
Arrangement fee:	£2,550

Early redemption penalty:	5% sum repaid until 30/11/2009, plus interest until the end of the month
Repayment method:	Interest only
Life insurance required:	No
Acceptable areas:	England, Wales and Scotland

Monthly costs

Initial monthly payment:	£368

Additional features

- The lender charges interest on a daily basis.
- The stand-alone rental cover requirement is 100%, using a notional rate of 6.24%.
- The minimum main income is £25,000.
- The minimum property value is up to £80,000.
- The scheme is fixed until 30/11/2009, then the Bank of England Base Rate (currently 5.75%), then plus 1.99% for the term.
- The maximum portfolio limit for any one customer is £5m.
- For new-build flats or apartments or those converted/renovated in the last 12 months, the maximum loan is 75%.

Lender:	**Chelsea Building Society**
Rate:	5.24% for two years
APR:	7.5%
Interest charged:	Annually
Product type:	Base Rate tracker
Arrangement fee:	£2,125
Early redemption penalty:	Fee of £175
Repayment method:	Interest only
Life insurance required:	No
Acceptable areas:	England, Wales and Scotland

Monthly costs

Initial monthly payment:	£372

Additional features

- The anticipated rent must be greater, or equal to, 100% of the interest payment based on the Standard Variable Rate for loans up to 65% LTV and 120% above 65% LTV.
- A maximum of 10 properties per applicant is allowed.
- The property must be self-contained and have no more than five bedrooms and no more than one kitchen.
- The letting must be on the basis of a single letting on the entire property and it must be on an assured shorthold tenancy. The term of the letting must be for no longer than six months.
- The scheme is the Bank of England Base Rate (currently 5.75%) with 0.21% discount for two years, then plus 1.99% for the term.
- The maximum aggregate loan on all rental properties is £2m.
- Buy-to-Let Standard Variable Rate – 7.74%.

Lender:	Saffron Building Society
Rate:	5.24% for two years
APR:	7.8%
Interest charged:	Daily
Product type:	Discount
Arrangement fee:	£2,125
Early redemption penalty:	2% of advance within two years
Repayment method:	Interest only
Life insurance required:	No
Acceptable areas:	England and Wales

Monthly costs

Initial monthly payment:	£372

Additional features

- Discount of 2.35% (Buy-to-Let Standard Variable Rate – 7.59%).

- A maximum of 10 properties per individual. The maximum lending is £5m. (Refer to lender for loans above £500,000.)

- The annual rental income must be at 115% of the interest payments.

- The lender charges interest on a daily basis.

- Not available to first-time buyers.

- Capital repayments up to 10% are allowed each year without penalty (a minimum of £500).

Lender:	The Mortgage Works
Rate:	5.29% until 31/12/2009
APR:	7.8%
Interest charged:	Annually
Product type:	Fixed
Arrangement fee:	£2,125
Early redemption penalty:	5% of sum repaid until 31/12/2009, plus £145 fee
Repayment method:	Interest only
Life insurance required:	No
Acceptable areas:	England, Wales and Scotland

Monthly costs

Initial monthly payment:	£375

Additional features

- The minimum valuation is £40,000.

- Gross monthly rent will be at least 120% of the monthly mortgage pay rate.

- Capital repayments up to 10% are allowed each year without penalty.

- For limited companies, expatriates and foreign nationals, the maximum LTV will be 5% less then shown (refer to lender for full details).

- Unlimited property portfolios are accepted, subject to £1.5m per property.
- The scheme is fixed until 31/12/2009, then the Bank of England Base Rate (currently 5.75%) plus 1.99%.
- The arrangement fee is 2.5% (with a minimum of £595).
- Foreign nationals are subject to 0.50% loading on rate (including revert to rate) and LTVs are reduced by 0.50%.
- The lender will only accept buy-to-let applications on properties aged over one year.

Lender:	Mortgage Express
Rate:	5.34% until 30/11/2009
APR:	7.7%
Interest charged:	Annually
Product type:	Fixed
Arrangement fee:	£2,125
Early redemption penalty:	5% interest until 30/11/2009, plus £250
Repayment method:	Interest only
Life insurance required:	No
Acceptable areas:	National coverage

Monthly costs

Initial monthly payment:	£379

Additional features

- The minimum lease allowed is 25 years on the maturity of the mortgage.
- DSS tenants, council or student tenants are not allowed.
- Applicants must have income, outside of rental income, of at least £20,000. However, the ability to repay the mortgage is based on the fact that the rental income must be at least 125% of the mortgage payment.

- The lender offers the facility to overpay and then drawdown funds as required.
- Full status with guarantees.
- The scheme is fixed until 30/11/2009, then the Bank of England Base Rate (currently 5.75%) plus 1.75%.
- A letting assessment fee of £60 will be made.
- The completion fee is 2.5% (with a minimum of £599).

80 per cent LTV

Lender:	Mortgage Trust
Rate:	5.46% until 31/01/2009
APR:	9.0%
Interest charged:	Annually
Product type:	Fixed
Arrangement fee:	£1,999
Early redemption penalty:	8% interest until the first anniversary or 31/01/2009, whichever is greater
Repayment method:	Interest only
Life insurance required:	No
Acceptable areas:	National coverage

Monthly costs

Initial monthly payment:	£364

Additional features

- The minimum valuation of any property is £50,000.
- The rental income must be at least equal to 125% of the monthly payment as calculated at 5.00%.
- The minimum lease allowed is 65 years at the start of the mortgage and 40 years remaining on the maturity of the mortgage.

- The scheme is fixed until 31/01/2009, then the rate charged is three-month LIBOR (currently 6.74%) plus 1.99%.
- Professional landlords and limited companies may be considered.
- Refer to the lender to consider multiple properties. Portfolio cases only – up to £5m at 85% LTV.
- Normal property exclusions, DSS tenants, freehold flats, maisonettes and holiday lets (refer to the lender for full details of the property exclusions).
- Full status, self-certifications and limited companies must have been trading for two years.
- Self-employed and self-certification applicants must have an accountant who has acted for the applicant for one year.
- Maximum LTV for expatriates – 70% up to £500,000.

Lender:	Giraffe
Rate:	5.47% until 31/08/2009
APR:	7.7%
Interest charged:	Annually
Product type:	Fixed
Arrangement fee:	£1,999
Early redemption penalty:	5% interest until 31/08/2009
Repayment method:	Interest only
Life insurance required:	No
Acceptable areas:	England, Wales, Scotland and Northern Ireland

Monthly costs

Initial monthly payment:	£365

Additional features

- The scheme is fixed until 31/08/2009, then the Bank of England Base Rate (currently 5.75%) plus 1.75%.

- The minimum valuation of any property is £40,000.
- DSS tenants, students (multiple tenancies (not houses in multiple occupation), maximum of four) allowed. No holiday lets or family members are allowed.
- No first-time buyers.
- Rental income yield is calculated at 118% of pay rate.
- The minimum income of £15,000 is required.
- A maximum of 15 properties per applicant is allowed. The total borrowing is £2.5m.
- Borrowers must be over 21.
- For employed applicants, last month's payslip and an employer's reference are required.
- For self-employed applicants, agreed tax assessments from the latest year, the latest year's audited accounts, prepared by a chartered, certified or authorised public accountant, are required. A letter is required from a chartered, certified or authorised public accountant confirming the applicant's salary or share of profit.
- The minimum loan for remortgage is £25,001.
- Capital repayments up to 10% are allowed each year without penalty (a minimum of £2,000).
- Excludes properties located in office blocks and local authority office conversions for ALL product types. Flats in converted office blocks and speculatively converted ex-local authority blocks are unacceptable.
- Part repayment administration fee – £50. Lending fee – £195 (due on completion, but the payment can be deferred until the mortgage is fully repaid). Full repayment mortgage release fee (currently £0).

Lender:	Lloyds TSB
Rate:	5.48% until 31/12/2009
APR:	8.0%
Interest charged:	Daily
Product type:	Base Rate tracker

Arrangement fee:	£2,000
Early redemption penalty:	3% of balance repaid until 31/12/2008, then 2% until 31/12/2009
Repayment method:	Interest only
Life insurance required:	No
Acceptable areas:	England, Wales and Scotland

Monthly costs

Initial monthly payment:	£366

Additional features

- Maximum LTV – 85% (65% LTV limit for new-build flats).

- Not more than nine let properties with LTSB Group (total loan amount of no more than £5m).

- Income of plus 50% of expected rental income or 100% of the monthly interest-only payment based on the Bank of England Base Rate (currently 5.75%) plus 1%.

- The property must be of good quality and A1 condition and it must not be divided into separate units.

- The property must be professionally managed.

- The property should be an assured shorthold tenancy.

- The lender charges interest on a daily basis.

- Buy-to-Let Standard Variable Rate – 7.75%.

- The scheme is the Bank of England Base Rate (currently 5.75%) with 0.27% discount until 31/12/2009.

- Product fee – 2.50%, plus upfront application fee of £99 (the application fee is valid for up to 12 months).

Lender:	Cheltenham & Gloucester
Rate:	5.48% until 31/12/2009
APR:	8.0%
Interest charged:	Daily

Product type:	Base Rate tracker
Arrangement fee:	£2,000
Early redemption penalty:	3% of balance repaid until 31/12/2008, then 2% until 31/12/2009
Repayment method:	Interest only
Life insurance required:	No
Acceptable areas:	England, Wales and Scotland

Monthly costs

Initial monthly payment:	£366

Additional features

- Maximum LTV – 85% (65% LTV limit for new-build flats).
- Not more than nine let properties with LTSB Group (total loan amount of no more than £5m).
- Income of plus 50% of expected rental income or 100% of the monthly interest-only payment based on the Bank of England Base Rate (currently 5.75%) plus 1%.
- The property must be of good quality and A1 condition and it must not be divided into separate units.
- The property must be professionally managed.
- The property should be an assured shorthold tenancy.
- The lender charges interest on a daily basis.
- Buy-to-Let Standard Variable Rate – 7.75%.
- The scheme is the Bank of England Base Rate (currently 5.75%) with 0.27% discount until 31/12/2009.
- Product fee – 2.50%, plus upfront application fee of £99 (the application fee is valid for up to 12 months).

Lender:	**Woolwich**
Rate:	5.49% until 02/12/2009
APR:	7.0%

Interest charged:	Annually
Product type:	Fixed
Arrangement fee:	£2,000
Early redemption penalty:	Six months' interest at the fixed rate or the Buy-to-Let Standard Variable Rate, whichever is higher, until 02/12/2009, plus a final repayment charge of £275
Repayment method:	Interest only
Life insurance required:	No
Acceptable areas:	National coverage

Monthly costs

Initial monthly payment:	£366

Additional features

- The minimum lease allowed is 50 years on the maturity of the mortgage.

- The lender will use an affordability calculation based on the anticipated rental income.

- The gross annual rental income must cover the annual mortgage interest payment by at least 125% for loans up to £500,000, by 140% for loans up to £750,000 and 150% up to £1m at a nominal rate of 5%.

- Mortgages taken out by special purpose vehicle limited companies (SPVs) or limited liability partnerships (LLPs) will continue to be assessed on the basis of 130% of the product pay rate, subject to LTV.

- Lending will be restricted to LTV 65% for applications where the borrower/director is a foreign national.

- The maximum aggregate borrowing is restricted to £5m. Clients wishing to exceed £1m must apply to the Woolwich Buy-to-Let Development Team.

- Application fees are payable upfront, reduced by £75 for repeat business.

- An assured shorthold tenancy (must be for a minimum term of six months and a maximum term of two years) to the following tenant types: a single household (e.g. individual/couple/ family unit) and a single assured shorthold tenancy for sharing students or professionals.

- Company and/or corporate lets (the minimum term of the lease is six months). Note: Premium leases, where all rent is paid in advance of the start of the tenancy, are not acceptable.

- College and/or university head tenancy schemes (the minimum term of the lease is six months).

- Leases to registered housing associations and/or local authorities (the minimum term of lease is six months).

- Letting to a related person of the applicant or directors/shareholders of a special purpose vehicle limited company (SPV) or letting to diplomatic tenants and or embassies or direct to DSS tenants, holiday lets, regulated and or sitting tenants, houses in multiple occupation (HMOs) and premium leases, where all rent is paid in advance at the start of the tenancy, are unacceptable.

- Capital repayments up to 10% are allowed each year without penalty.

- The scheme is fixed until 02/12/2009, then the Bank of England Base Rate (currently 5.75%) plus 0.95% for the term.

- The application fee is 2.5% (a minimum of £595).

- For remortgages only: a free non-disclosed valuation through the lender's nominated valuer and free remortgage legal fees through the lender's nominated solicitor or cashback.

Lender:	Barclays
Rate:	5.49% until 02/12/2009
APR:	7.0%
Interest charged:	Annually
Product type:	Fixed
Arrangement fee:	£2,000
Early redemption penalty:	Six months' interest at the fixed rate

	or the Buy-to-Let Standard Variable Rate, whichever is higher, until 02/12/2009, plus a final repayment charge of £275
Repayment method:	Interest only
Life insurance required:	No
Acceptable areas:	National coverage

Monthly costs

Initial monthly payment:	£366

Additional features

- The minimum lease allowed is 50 years on the maturity of the mortgage.

- The lender will use an affordability calculation based on the anticipated rental income.

- The gross annual rental income must cover the annual mortgage interest payment by at least 125% for loans up to £500,000, by 140% for loans up to £750,000 and 150% up to £1m at a nominal rate of 5%.

- Mortgages taken out by special purpose vehicle limited companies (SPVs) or limited liability partnerships (LLPs) will continue to be assessed on the basis of 130% of the product pay rate, subject to LTV.

- Lending will be restricted to LTV 65% for applications where the borrower/director is a foreign national.

- The maximum aggregate borrowing is restricted to £5m.

- The application fees are payable upfront, reduced by £75 for repeat business.

- An assured shorthold tenancy (must be for a minimum term of six months and a maximum term of two years) to the following tenant types: a single household (e.g. individual/couple/ family unit) and a single assured shorthold tenancy for sharing students or professionals.

- Company and/or corporate lets (the minimum term of the lease is six months). Note: Premium leases, where all rent is paid in advance of the start of the tenancy, are not acceptable.

- College and/or university head tenancy schemes (the minimum term of the lease is six months).

- Leases to registered housing associations and/or local authorities (the minimum term of the lease is six months).

- Letting to a related person of the applicant or directors/shareholders of a special purpose vehicle limited company (SPV) or letting to diplomatic tenants and or embassies or direct to DSS tenants, holiday lets, regulated and or sitting tenants, houses in multiple occupation (HMOs) and premium leases, where all rent is paid in advance at the start of the tenancy, are unacceptable.

- Capital repayments up to 10% are allowed each year without penalty.

- The scheme is fixed until 02/12/2009, then the Bank of England Base Rate (currently 5.75%) plus 0.95% for the term.

- The application fee is 2.5% (a minimum of £595).

- For remortgages only: free a non-disclosed valuation through the lender's nominated valuer and free remortgage legal fees through the lender's nominated solicitor or cashback.

Lender:	Derbyshire Building Society
Rate:	5.49% until 30/11/2009
APR:	7.2%
Interest charged:	Daily
Product type:	Fixed
Arrangement fee:	£2,000
Early redemption penalty:	5% until 30/11/2009 of the amount repaid
Repayment method:	Interest only
Life insurance required:	No
Acceptable areas:	England and Wales

Monthly costs

Initial monthly payment: £366

Additional features

- Intermediary only.
- A maximum of 10 properties per applicant (£5m in total).
- The main applicant must be aged 25, been in permanent employment for 12 months or self-employed for three years.
- Income or net profit of £25,000 or more is required.
- The gross monthly rental must be at least 100% up to 75% LTV, 110% up to 80% LTV and 115% up to 85% LTV, of monthly interest at initial payable rate (an income option is available – refer to lender for full details).
- Lettings must be on an assured shorthold tenancy.
- Properties not acceptable: ex-local authority flats, flats over commercial premises, one-bedroom flats, any multi-occupation property, student lets, DSS lets and flats in blocks over four storeys.
- The lender charges interest on a daily basis.
- The lender doesn't require life policies to be deposited with the title deeds or to know how an interest-only mortgage is to be repaid at the end of the mortgage repayment period.
- Capital raising is acceptable on this product for improvements or the purchase of a further investment property (interest at 0.50% below SRV), maximum LTV in these circumstances is 75%. The lender must provide any mortgage on any additional property.
- Capital repayments up to 10% are allowed each year without penalty.
- An arrangement fee of 2.5% (a non-refundable booking fee of £95 is included to be paid upfront).
- For loans above £500,000 – refer to lender.
- The scheme is fixed until 30/11/2009, then the Bank of England Base Rate (currently 5.75%) plus 1.25% for the term.
- Mortgages by ex-pats allowed.

75 per cent LTV

Lender:	**Stroud & Swindon**
Rate:	4.89%
APR:	6.5%
Product type:	Fixed
Period:	31/05/2008
Arrangement fee:	£740
Early redemption penalty:	3%, then 2% of outstanding balance until 31/05/2008, plus £125
Repayment options:	Capital interest or interest only
Life insurance required:	No
Acceptable areas:	England and Wales

Monthly costs

Monthly mortgage payment – interest only:	£305.62

Additional features

- Only available direct with the lender.
- The minimum valuation of any property is £75,000.
- The minimum lease allowed is 50 years on the maturity of the mortgage.
- DSS tenants, council or student tenants are not allowed.
- Capital repayments up to 25% are allowed without penalty.
- The lender will use income multiples, less existing commitments plus 130% of annual rent to determine maximum borrowings (additional income can also be used).
- A maximum loan of £250,000 per property. The total maximum borrowing allowed is £500,000 over a portfolio of three properties.
- Discounted legal fees for remortgaging are available. These include a free valuation (on properties valued at £600,000 or less).

- Available to individuals who have been UK residents for three years and currently own their homes.
- The fee shown is made up from a £245 reservation fee and a £495 completion fee.

Lender:	Woolwich
Rate:	4.89%
APR:	5.7%
Product type:	Fixed
Period:	02/06/2008
Arrangement fee:	£1,125
Early redemption penalty:	Six months' interest at the fixed rate or the Buy-to-Let Standard Variable Rate, whichever is higher, until 02/06/2008, plus a final repayment charge of £275
Repayment options:	Capital interest or interest only
Life insurance required:	No
Acceptable areas:	National coverage

Monthly costs

Monthly mortgage payment – interest only:	£305.62

Additional features

- The minimum lease allowed is 50 years on the maturity of the mortgage.
- The lender will use an affordability calculation based on the anticipated rental income.
- The gross annual rental income must cover the annual mortgage interest payment by at least 130% for loans up to £500,000, by 140% for loans up to £750,000, and 150% up to £1m.
- Lending will be restricted to LTV 65% for applications where the borrower/director is a foreign national.

- The maximum aggregate borrowing is restricted to £5m. Clients wishing to exceed £1m must apply to the Woolwich Buy-to-Let Development Team.
- Application fees are payable upfront, reduced by £75 for repeat business.
- An assured shorthold tenancy (must be for a minimum term of six months and a maximum term of two years) to the following tenant types: a single household (e.g. individual/couple/family unit), a single assured shorthold tenancy for sharing students or professionals.
- Company and/or corporate lets (the minimum term of the lease is six months). Note: Premium leases, where all rent is paid in advance of the start of the tenancy, are not acceptable.
- College and/or university head tenancy schemes (the minimum term of the lease is six months).
- Leases to registered housing associations and/or local authorities (the minimum term of the lease is six months).
- Letting to a related person of the applicant or directors/shareholders of a special purpose vehicle limited company (SPV) or letting to diplomatic tenants and/or embassies or direct to DSS tenants, holiday lets, regulated and/or sitting tenants, houses in multiple occupation (HMOs), and premium leases, where all rent is paid in advance at the start of the tenancy, are unacceptable.
- Capital repayments up to 10% are allowed each year without penalty.
- Available to private individuals and special purpose vehicle limited companies (SPVs).
- The scheme is fixed until 02/06/2008, then the Bank Base Rate Tracker (currently 4.50%) plus 0.95% for the term.

Lender:	Leek United
Rate:	4.99%
APR:	6.3%
Product type:	Discount
Period:	3 years

Arrangement fee:	£495
Early redemption penalty:	5% within three years of the amount repaid
Repayment options:	Capital interest or interest only
Life insurance required:	No
Acceptable areas:	England and Wales

Monthly costs

Monthly mortgage payment – interest only:	£311.88

Additional features

- No studio, freehold and ex-council flats, bedsits, DSS tenants, students, houses converted into flats, multiple occupation properties, property developers and professional landlords.
- Acceptable property type: houses and purpose-built flats (a maximum of four storeys).
- Rental income to be at least 130% of mortgage interest at the lender (to be calculated at pay rate).
- The lender uses an affordability scale incorporating income multiples and property rental.
- It can accommodate small portfolios of properties (a maximum of five).
- 1.50% discount.
- A loyalty bonus applies after five years (currently 0.25%).
- Capital repayments up to 10% are allowed each year without penalty.
- Properties to be let on assured shorthold tenancies for a maximum of 12 months (only one per property/no charge to approve initial tenancy agreement).
- £300 cashback.
- Interest calculated daily.
- Free valuation on a property valued up to £500,000.

- The fee shown is £100 payable upfront and £395 non-refundable (deducted from advance).

Lender:	Woolwich
Rate:	4.99%
APR:	5.9%
Product type:	Base Rate tracker
Period:	1 year
Arrangement fee:	£495
Early redemption penalty:	Six months' interest within three years at the charging rate, plus a final repayment charge of £275
Repayment options:	Capital interest or interest only
Life insurance required:	No
Acceptable areas:	National coverage

Monthly costs

Monthly mortgage payment – interest only:	£311.88

Additional features

- The minimum lease allowed is 50 years on the maturity of the mortgage.
- The lender will use an affordability calculation based on the anticipated rental income.
- The gross annual rental income must cover the annual mortgage interest payment by at least 130% for loans up to £500,000, by 140% for loans up to £750,000, and 150% up to £1m.
- The scheme is the Bank Base Rate Tracker (currently 4.50%) plus 0.49% for one year, then plus 1.20% for the term.
- Lending will be restricted to LTV 65% for applications where the borrower/director is a foreign national.
- The maximum aggregate borrowing is restricted to £5m. Clients

wishing to exceed £1m must apply to the Woolwich Buy-to-Let Development Team.

- The application fees are payable upfront, reduced by £75 for repeat business.
- An assured shorthold tenancy (must be for a minimum term of six months and a maximum term of two years) to the following tenant types: a single household (e.g. individual/couple/family unit), a single assured shorthold tenancy for sharing students or professionals.
- Company and/or corporate lets (the minimum term of the lease is six months). Note: Premium leases, where all rent is paid in advance of the start of the tenancy, are not acceptable.
- College and/or university head tenancy schemes (the minimum term of the lease is six months).
- Leases to registered housing associations and/or local authorities (the minimum term of the lease is six months).
- Letting to a related person of the applicant or directors/shareholders of a special purpose vehicle limited company (SPV) or letting to diplomatic tenants and/or embassies or direct to DSS tenants, holiday lets, regulated and/or sitting tenants, houses in multiple occupation (HMOs), and premium leases, where all rent is paid in advance at the start of the tenancy, are unacceptable.
- Available to private individuals and special purpose vehicle limited companies (SPVs).
- Capital repayments up to 10% are allowed each year without penalty.

Lender:	Bath Building Society
Rate:	4.99%
APR:	6.8%
Product type:	Discount
Period:	2 years
Arrangement fee:	£400
Early redemption penalty:	3% within two years of capital repayment, plus £135
Repayment options:	Capital interest or interest only

Life insurance required:	No
Acceptable areas:	England and Wales

Monthly costs

Monthly mortgage payment – interest only:	£311.88

Additional features

- The minimum property value is £60,000.
- The rental income to cover interest at 7%.
- The minimum income is £15,000 (one applicant).
- The maximum loan is negotiable.
- The lender will consider multiple occupancy, company and student lets.
- The minimum age is 25. There is no maximum, subject to income in retirement.
- The scheme is 1.51% discount for the first year, then 0.60% discount in the second year.

Lender:	Bank of Scotland Mort Dir
Rate:	5.09%
APR:	6.6%
Product type:	Fixed
Period:	31/03/2009
Arrangement fee:	£599
Early redemption penalty:	3% until 31/03/2009
Repayment options:	Capital interest or interest only
Life insurance required:	Yes
Acceptable areas:	National coverage

Monthly costs

Monthly mortgage payment – interest only:	£318.12

Additional features

- The minimum valuation is £50,000.
- The minimum age of applicants is 25.
- The maximum term is 40 years.
- A maximum of five properties or £5m overall. Lending subject to a maximum of 10 properties across the HBOS group.
- Multiple occupancies and bedsits are excluded.
- Annualised rental income must cover 125% of the annual mortgage repayment.
- The ability to overpay, underpay and take payment holidays.

65 per cent LTV

Lender:	Standard Life Bank
Rate:	4.19%
APR:	6.5%
Product type:	Discount
Period:	1 year
Arrangement fee:	£350
Early redemption penalty:	Five months' gross interest at the variable rate within three years, plus £185 for the term
Repayment options:	Capital interest or interest only
Life Insurance required:	No
Acceptable areas:	England, Wales, Scotland and Northern Ireland

Monthly costs

Monthly mortgage payment – interest only:	£226.96

Additional features

- The minimum age of the applicant is 25 years. The maximum age is 70 years.
- A minimum employment income of £20,000 single or £30,000 joint, excluding rental income.
- The maximum total of loans is £1m (a maximum of £400,000 for a single property).
- Up to 10 rental properties.
- Overpayments allowed (£1,000 minimum lump sums).
- Up to two payment holidays are allowed per year per property.
- The lender charges interest on a daily basis.
- The annual rental income must equal at least 130% of monthly interest based on the interest rate of 6.44%.
- A 2.25% discount off the Buy-to-Let Variable Rate of 6.44%.
- Self-certification allowed for loans of less than 50% LTVs.
- Guarantor applications to a maximum of 65% LTV.
- Professional landlords to a maximum of 65% LTV.
- Where the primary source of income is via letting or property development to a maximum of 65% LTV.
- Customers whose mortgage term takes them beyond the age of 65 to a maximum of 65% LTV with no income verification required.
- If the buy-to-let mortgage is used to rent to a family member, the mortgage may be regulated by the FSA regime. In this circumstance, please refer to the lender for an illustration.
- An arrangement fee (of £350) for a single property. The arrangement for multiple is £500.

Lender:	Coventry
Rate:	5.10%
APR:	5.4%
Product type:	Variable
Period:	25 years

Arrangement fee:	£725
Early redemption penalty:	None
Repayment options:	Capital interest or interest only
Life insurance required:	No
Acceptable areas:	England, Wales and mainland Scotland

Monthly costs

Monthly mortgage payment – interest only:	£276.25

Additional features

- Guaranteed to be no more than 2.00% above the Standard Variable Rate.
- The property must be let on an assured shorthold tenancy.
- It isn't available to companies or partnerships.
- The minimum annual income for the main earner is £20,000.
- Employed applicants must be in permanent employment and have been so continuously for 12 months.
- The self-employed must be verified via their last two years' accounts.
- Flats in blocks of no more than five storeys are allowed. The maximum loan is 65%.
- Applicants must be aged 25 or above.
- The monthly rental must be at least 130% of the monthly mortgage interest.
- No studio flats or properties converted for multi-occupancy, or students lets are allowed.
- A maximum of five rental properties is allowed. The maximum loan amount is £500,000 in total.
- Where an existing customer has a residential mortgage and buys another property (letting out the original), the lender will allow up to 80% LTV on the new residential property.
- A maximum of a three-month payment break per year (by approval).

A facility for overpayments.

- A free valuation (with a maximum of £680).

- An arrangement fee (with a total of £725) is made up of a £250 booking fee and a £475 arrangement fee.

- A free remortgage transfer service is available which includes legal fees if the lender's nominated solicitor is used (alternatively, a £200 contribution). Scottish cases will only receive a £200 contribution.

- The lender charges interest on a daily basis.

Lender:	Irish Permanent
Rate:	5.15%
APR:	5.8%
Product type:	Base Rate tracker
Period:	31/10/2007
Arrangement fee:	£325
Early redemption penalty:	5% of redeeming balance until 31/10/2007
Repayment options:	Capital interest or interest only
Life insurance required:	No
Acceptable areas:	Mainland England, Wales and Northern Ireland

Monthly costs

Monthly mortgage payment – interest only:	£278.96

Additional features

- The minimum valuation of any property is £40,000 (a minimum of £50,000 for one-bedroom flats/maisonettes).

- The minimum lease allowed is 35 years on the maturity of the mortgage.

- The minimum arrangement fee is £300.

- The applicants must be resident and paying UK tax for a minimum of three years.
- The applicants must be existing homeowners with an outstanding mortgage or be limited companies/property developers/commercial landlords.
- The rental income must be at least 125% of the mortgage interest.
- DSS tenants, council or student tenants are not allowed.
- The scheme is the Bank of England Base Rate (currently 4.50%) plus 0.65% until 31/10/2007, then plus 1.24%.
- An Assured Shorthold Tenancy Agreement or company letting agreement is required.
- CCJs are considered. A maximum of two CCJs to a combined value of £500 and they must be satisfied for at least two years.
- Capital repayments up to 20% are allowed each year without penalty.

Lender:	Woolwich
Rate:	5.19%
APR:	5.6%
Product type:	Fixed
Period:	02/06/2008
Arrangement fee:	£195
Early redemption penalty:	Six months' interest at the fixed rate or the Buy-to-Let Standard Variable Rate, whichever is higher, plus £300 until 02/06/2008 plus a final repayment charge of £275
Repayment options:	Capital interest or interest only
Life insurance required:	No
Acceptable areas:	National coverage

Monthly costs

Monthly mortgage payment – interest only:	£281.12

Additional features

- The minimum lease allowed is 50 years on the maturity of the mortgage.

- The lender will use an affordability calculation based on the anticipated rental income.

- The gross annual rental income must cover the annual mortgage interest payment by at least 130% for loans up to £500,000, by 140% for loans up to £750,000, and 150% up to £1m.

- Lending will be restricted to LTV 65% for applications where the borrower/director is a foreign national.

- The maximum aggregate borrowing is restricted to £5m. Clients wishing to exceed £1m must apply to the Woolwich Buy-to-Let Development Team.

- Remortgages only with free non-disclosed valuation through the lender's nominated valuer and free remortgage legal fees through the lender's nominated solicitor.

- Application fees are payable upfront, reduced by £75 for repeat business.

- An assured shorthold tenancy (must be for a minimum term of six months and a maximum term of two years) to the following tenant types: a single household (e.g. individual/couple/family unit), a single assured shorthold tenancy for sharing students or professionals.

- Company and/or corporate lets (the minimum term of the lease is six months). Note: Premium leases, where all rent is paid in advance of the start of the tenancy, are not acceptable.

- College and/or university head tenancy schemes (the minimum term of the lease is six months).

- Leases to registered housing associations and/or local authorities (the minimum term of the lease is six months).

- Letting to a related person of the applicant or directors/shareholders of a special purpose vehicle limited company (SPV) or letting to diplomatic tenants and/or embassies or direct to DSS tenants, holiday lets, regulated and/or sitting tenants, houses in multiple occupation (HMOs) and premium leases, where all rent is paid in advance at the start of the tenancy, are unacceptable.

- Capital repayments up to 10% are allowed each year without penalty.
- Available to private individuals.
- The scheme is fixed until 02/06/2008, then the Bank of England Base Rate (currently 4.50%) plus 0.95% for the term.

List of property websites

The list of websites below enables you to search for properties in the area that interests you. All these sites direct you ultimately to the estate agent who is selling the property. There are also rental sites included in this list, so you can keep abreast of the current market rental values of properties you have or are currently interested in.

I personally use rightmove.co.uk, ukpropertyshop.com and home.co.uk to find my properties. These sites seem professionally run and have a large database of properties for sale.

I would suggest that you search for properties listed in the hotspots detailed in part 6 of this chapter.

Sales and rental websites

1. www.accommodatingcompany.co.uk
2. www.ashtons.co.uk
3. www.bainprop.co.uk
4. www.bansalestates.co.uk
5. www.bennettjones.co.uk
6. www.cdproperty.co.uk
7. www.chesterton.co.uk
8. www.claridges-estates.co.uk
9. www.dauntons.co.uk
10. www.davisestates.co.uk
11. www.dmea.co.uk
12. www.excel-property.co.uk
13. www.fish4homes.co.uk

14. www.foxtons.co.uk
15. www.globalmart.co.uk
16. www.halfapercent.com
17. www.hamiltonbrooks.co.uk
18. www.haylingproperty.co.uk
19. www.home.co.uk
20. www.home-sale.co.uk
21. www.hotproperty.co.uk
22. www.housemarket.co.uk
23. www.housesearchuk.co.uk
24. www.houseweb.co.uk
25. www.howards.co.uk
26. www.jparissteele.co.uk
27. www.lakewood-properties.co.uk
28. www.londonshome.co.uk
29. www.lookproperty.co.uk
30. www.milburys.co.uk
31. www.naea.co.uk
32. www.net-lettings.co.uk
33. www.newey.co.uk
34. www.nicholasirwin.co.uk
35. www.numberone4property.co.uk
36. www.palacegate.co.uk
37. www.palmsagency.co.uk
38. www.paramount-properties.co.uk
39. www.primelocation.com
40. www.propertyfinder.com
41. www.property-go.co.uk
42. www.propertymatters.co.uk
43. www.propertyworld.com
44. www.p4L.co.uk
45. www.rentalsandsales.co.uk
46. www.rightmove.co.uk
47. www.sequencehome.co.uk
48. www.shobrook.co.uk
49. www.stewartwatson.co.uk
50. www.stonegateonline.co.uk
51. www.thehousehunter.co.uk
52. www.thelondonoffice.co.uk

53. www.themovechannel.com
54. www.ukpropertyshop.co.uk
55. www.vebra.com
56. www.your-move.co.uk

Sales only websites

1. www.daltonsproperty.com
2. www.fairview.co.uk
3. www.gatehouseestates.co.uk
4. www.golfhomes.co.uk
5. www.homepages.co.uk
6. www.homesalez.com
7. www.homeselluk.com
8. www.housenet.co.uk
9. www.smartestates.com
10. www.smartnewhomes.com
11. www.tspc.co.uk
12. www.villagategroup.com
13. www.wisemove.co.uk

Rentals only websites

1. www.assuredproprentals.co.uk
2. www.cambridgeletting.co.uk
3. www.citylets.co.uk
4. www.faulknerproperty.co.uk
5. www.flemingpropertyrentals.co.uk
6. www.homelet.co.uk
7. www.letters.co.uk
8. www.lettingsearch.co.uk
9. www.lettingweb.com
10. www.mossoak.co.uk
11. www.simplyrent.co.uk
12. www.studentpad.co.uk
13. www.torent.co.uk

Mortgage brokers

A local mortgage broker can be found quite easily through the *Yellow Pages* or www.yell.com. You can use my mortgage broker if you wish. Her name is Liz Syms and she can be contacted on Tel: (01708) 443 334; Fax: (01708) 470 043. If you mention the reference 'Ajay Ahuja', you'll receive a discount on her fees of up to 50 per cent. She is very good – this is why I use her! If not, I suggest you go for a buy-to-let specialist mortgage broker. These can be found from the following websites. You have to specify a buy-to-let specialist when searching:

www.ifap.org.uk and www.unbiased.co.uk

IFA Promotion Ltd, 2nd Floor, 117 Farringdon Road, London, EC1R 3BX. Tel: (0800) 085 3250

www.ifawindow.co.uk

Web-based only.

www.searchifa.co.uk

Unit 8, Alpha Business Park, Travellers Close, Hatfield, AL9 7NT. Tel: (01707) 251 111

List of accommodation projects

Accommodation projects can find tenants, guarantee and collect the rent and liaise with the tenants on your behalf. Basically, they can act like an agent for you, but the great thing is that they provide their services for FREE! The reason they can provide them for free is because they are non-profit organisations or charities. Consequently, it would be beneficial to donate to the project you use intermittently in order to encourage good relations.

England (North)

Cheshire

Chester Aid to the Homeless
Rent Deposit Scheme, Watergate House, 85 Watergate Street,

Chester, CH1 2LF.
Tel: (01244) 314 834
Email: robert.bisset@cath.org.uk
Web: www.homelessnessinchester.org

EPNBC Rent Deposit Scheme

Ellesmere Port and Neston Borough Council, 4 Civic Way, Ellesmere
Port, Chester, CH65 0BE.
Tel: (0151) 356 6789
Website: www.epnbc.gov.uk

Cumbria

DiGS (Cumbria)

Tangier Building, Greggs Lane, Whitehaven, Cumbria, CA28 7UH.
Tel: (01946) 694 166
Email: digs.cumbria@googlemail.com

Derbyshire

Chesterfield Borough Council

Homelessness Service, Town Hall, Rose Hill, Chesterfield, S40 1LP.
Tel: (01246) 345 826
Email: diane.price@chesterfield.gov.uk

SmartMove (Derbyshire)

Derbyshire Housing Aid, Glad Tidings Hall, 33 Boyer Street, Derby,
DE22 3TB.
Tel: (01332) 867 810
Web: www.housingaid.org.uk

Durham

Centrepoint North East Rental Deposit Guarantee Scheme

Miners Hall, Red Hill, Durham, DH1 4BB.
Tel: (0191) 384 4033
Email: adavison@centrepoint.org
Website: www.centrepoint.org

Darlington Bond Scheme

Grange Road Baptist Church, Grange Road, Darlington, DL1 5NH.
Tel: (01325) 467 617

Email: bondscheme@darlingtoncharity.fsnet.co.uk
Website: www.darlingtoncharity.fsnet.co.uk/index.html

Greater Manchester

Salford City Council

Private Sector Team, Housing Advice Support, Crompton House, 100 Chorley Road, Swinton, Salford, M6 5FW.
Tel: (0161) 793 2020
Website: www.salford.gov.uk

The Bond Board Ltd.

41 Mawdsley Street, Bolton, BL1 1LN.
Tel: (01204) 366 328 (Access through Housing Advice, Tel: (01204) 335 900)
Email: info@thebondboard.org.uk
Website: www.thebondboard.org.uk

Hartlepool

Hartlepool Housing Advice & Tenancy Support Service

Hartlepool Citizens Advice Bureau, 87 Park Road, Hartlepool, TS26 9HP.
Tel: (01429) 277 030
Email: team@htss.fsnet.co.uk
Website: www.hartlepool.cab.co.uk

Kingston-upon-Hull

Humbercare Ltd

Single Persons Homeless & Housing Project, 81 Beverley Road, Hull, HU3 1XR.
Tel: (01482) 586 633
Email: jane-anne@humbercare1.karoo.co.uk

Lancashire

Blackburn with Darwen Rent Deposit Bond Scheme

Housing Needs Section, Room 102, The Old Town Hall, Blackburn, BB1 7DY.
Tel: (01254) 585 444

Blackpool Council
South King Street, Blackpool, FY1 4TR.
Tel: (01253) 477 556
Email: liz.kenyon@blackpool.gov.uk

Bury Bond Board
19 Knowfley Street, Bury, BL9 0ST.
Tel: (0161) 761 6166

Face-To-Face
14 St Davids Road South, St Annes On Sea, Lytham St Annes, FY8 1TB.
Tel: (01253) 720 270
Email: markmoir@f2ffylde.fsnet.co.uk

Lancaster and District YMCA
Young Person's Deposit Guarantee Scheme, Heart of the City, Fleet
Square, Lancaster, LA1 1HA.
Tel: (0152) 432 737
Email: ymcalancaster@btconnect.com
Website: www.lancasterymca.co.uk

Rochdale Bond Board
Strategic Housing Services, PO Box 423, Rochdale, OL16 1WB.
Tel: (01706) 926 680

SmartMove (Chorley)
Help the Homeless, 45 Clifford Street, Chorley, PR7 1SE.
Tel: (01257) 273 320
Email: sandra@helpthehomeless.org.uk

South Ribble Churches Rent Guarantee Scheme
South Ribble Borough Council, Civic Centre, West Paddock, Leyland,
Preston, PR25 1DH.
Tel: (01772) 625 361
Website : www.southribble.gov.uk

Leicestershire

Leicester City Council
Housing Options Manager, New Walk Centre, Welford Place, Leicester,
LE1 6ZG.
Tel: (0116) 252 6850

Lincolnshire

SmartMove (Scunthorpe)
PO Box 210, 4A Queensway Industrial Estate, Dunlop Way, Scunthorpe, DN16 3XR.
Tel: (01724) 856 414
Email: tracy.hotham@virgin.net

South Holland District Council
Rent in Advance and Deposit Scheme, Priory Road, Spalding, PE11 2XQ.
Tel: (01775) 761 161
Email: pwaller@sholland.gov.uk
Website: www.sholland.gov.uk

Manchester

RentWise
1–5 West Street, Clayton, Manchester, M11 4EF.
Tel: (0161) 230 8879
Email: Rentwise@manchester.gov.uk
Website: www.manchester.gov.uk/housing/privatesector/rentwise/nodeposit.htm

Merseyside

Nugent Care
Deposit Guarantee and Supported Housing Scheme (RDS), 99 Edge Lane, Liverpool, L7 2PE.
Tel: (0151) 261 2000
Website: www.nugentcare.org

SmartMove (Southport)
Southport Housing Centre, 68 Eastbank Street, Southport, PR8 1ES.
Tel: (01704) 501 256
Email: sylvia.byron@lightforlife.plus.com

North Yorkshire

EasyLet
York CAB, 3 Blossom Street, York, YO24 1AU.
Tel: (01904) 623 648
Email: bgs@yorkcab.org.uk

Foundation Housing
Unit 1, Carlton Business Park, Carlton New Road, Skipton, BD23 2DE.
Tel: (01756) 701 110
Email: skipton@foundationhousing.org.uk

Ryedale Bond Guarantee Scheme
Ryedale District Council, Ryedale House, Old Malton, Malton, YO17 7HH.
Tel: (01653) 600 666
Email: kim.robertshaw@ryedale.gov.uk

Northamptonshire

Borough Council of Wellingborough
Tithe Barn Road, Wellingborough, NN8 1BN.
Tel: (01933) 229 777

Bridge Accommodation Project
Citizens' Advice Bureau, 2B High Street, Wellingborough, NN8 4HR.
Tel: (01933) 229 781
Email: paulc@bridge.wellingboroughcab.org.uk

CAN Homeless Action Team
The Maple Centre, PO Box 5164, 37 Ash Street, Northampton, NN1 3ZP.
Tel: (01604) 250 678
Email: rob.walkham@can.org.uk

Nottinghamshire

Moveahead
Mansfield District Council Bond Guarantee Scheme, 65 Westgate, Mansfield, NG18 1RU.
Tel: (01623) 463 463
Email: vpalmer@Mansfield.gov.uk
Website: www.moveahead.ms

Shropshire

Homeless in Oswestry Action Partnership (HOAP)
Centre North West, Oak Street, Oswestry, SY11 1LW.
Tel: (01691) 650 850
Website: www.hoap.org.uk

Housing Young People in Shrewsbury

Roy Fletcher Centre, 12–17 Cross Hill, Shrewsbury, SY1 1JE.
Tel: (01743) 341 900
Email: hypshousing@yahoo.co.uk
Website: www.hyps.org.uk

Shrewsbury Homes for All

First Floor Offices, 2/3 Wyle Cop, Shrewsbury, SY1 1UT.
Tel: (01743) 231 415
Email: office@shfa.fsnet.co.uk

South Yorkshire

Action Housing and Support Ltd

Bond Guarantee Scheme, 40 Duke Street, Doncaster, DN1 3EA.
Tel: (01302) 561 254

Housing Solutions

2nd Floor, Howden House, 1 Union Street, Sheffield, S1 2SH.
Tel: (0114) 205 3112

Robond Ltd

Floor 2, Municiple Offices, Smith Street, Rochdale, OL16 1LQ.
Tel: (01709) 926 680
Email: david.robond@btconnect.com

SmartMove (Sheffield)

NOMAD – SmartMove, 90–92 West Street, Sheffield, S1 4EP.
Tel: (0114) 273 8805
Email: smartmove@nomadsheffield.co.uk

SmartMove 2 Barnsley

Action Housing Association, 34 Victoria Road, Barnsley, S70 2BU.
Tel: (01226) 209 333
Email: jacqueline.garrison@actionhousinguk.org

Staffordshire

Cannock Chase Churches Housing Coalition

Housing & Health Advice Centre, 29–31 Park Road, Cannock, WS11 1JN.
Tel: (01543) 577 572
Email: ejbrooks@talktalk.net

Teesside

SmartMove (Teesside)
THAG Information and Resource Centre, 157 Albert Road,
Middlesbrough, TS1 2PS.
Tel: (01642) 224 772
Email: thag@talk21.com

Tyne & Wear

CATalyst
Resource Centre, Oxford Street, Whitley Bay, NE26 1AD.
Tel: (0191) 253 6161
Email: info@catalyst-ne.org
Website: www.catalyst-ne.org

West Midlands

Walsall Rent Guarantee Scheme
PO Box 1427, Walsall, WS4 2YT.
Tel: (01922) 746 798

West Yorkshire

Kirklees Bond Bank
1st Floor, Standard House, Half Moon Street, Huddersfield, HD1 2JF.
Tel: (01484) 223 926
Email: david.mariani@chaskirklees.org.uk
Website: www.kirkleesadvice.org.uk

SmartMove (Calderdale)
Calderdale Bond Scheme Ltd, 9 Portland Place, Halifax, HX1 2JQ.
Tel: (01422) 361 515
Email: sarah@calderdalesmartmove.org.uk

Wakefield Rent Deposit Scheme
2nd Floor, Queens House, Queen Row, Market Street, Wakefield,
WF1 1DF.
Tel: (01924) 304 575
Email: info@wrds.org.uk

England (South)

Bedfordshire

Bedford Borough Council

Housing Advice Service, Town Hall, St Paul's Square, Bedford, MK40 1SJ.
Tel: (01234) 221 776
Email: dparker@bedford.gov.uk
Website: www.bedford.gov.uk

Bristol

Bristol City Council Deposit Bond Scheme

The Hub, 13–17 Cumberland Street, St Pauls, Bristol, BS2 8NL.
Tel: (0117) 914 1209
Email: felicity_marechal@bristol-city.gov.uk or karen_wilkin@bristol-city.gov.uk

Buckinghamshire

Shelter Deposit Scheme

The Food Centre, 793 Avebury Boulevard, Milton Keynes, MK9 3JT.
Tel: (01908) 667 599
Email: sheltermkdeposits@shelter.org.uk

Wycombe Rent Deposit Guarantee Scheme

52 Frogmore, High Wycombe, HP13 5DG.
Tel: (01494) 528 557
Email: phil@wycrent.freeserve.co.uk

Cambridgeshire

Cambridge City Rent Deposit Scheme

Cambridge City Council, 44 St Andrews Street, Cambridge, CB2 3AS.
Tel: (01223) 457 931
Email: rob.henrique@cambridge.gov.uk

King Street Housing Society Ltd

Rent Deposit Partnership, 89 King Street, Cambridge, CB1 1LD.
Tel: (01223) 312 294
Email: info@kingstreeths.org.uk
Website: www.kingstreeths.org.uk

Cornwall

Accommodation Bonds for Cornwall
Stonham Housing with Care, PO Box 113, Redruth, TR15 2YP.
Tel: (01209) 216 166
Email: eddy.o'connor@homegroup.org.uk

SHARE St Austell
1 Biddicks Court, St Austell, PL25 5EW.
Tel: (01726) 691 44

SmartMove (North Cornwall and Caradon)
St Petroc's Society, PO Box 97, Bodmin, PL31 2WY.
Tel: (01872) 797 34
Email: rbower.stpetroc@btconnect.com
Website: www.stpetrocs.org.uk

Devon

Churches Housing Action Team (Mid Devon) Ltd
28 Gold Street, Tiverton, EX16 6PY.
Tel: (01884) 255 606
Email: theoffice@chatmid.co.uk

Newton Abbot Rent Deposit Guarantee Scheme
13 Wilbraham Court, Higher Woodway Road, Teignmouth, TQ14 8WE.
Tel: (01626) 770 578
Email: williamr.b@ntlworld.com

Plymouth Access to Housing
Midland House, Notte Street, Plymouth, PL1 2EJ.
Tel: (01752) 305 955
Website: www.plymouthpath.org

SmartMove (Exeter)
Exeter Homeless Action Group, Palace Gatehouse, Exeter, EX1 1HX.
Tel: (01392) 430 228
Email: smartmove@ehag.org.uk
Website: www.ehag.org.uk

SmartMove (North Devon)
North Devon Housing Society, 109 High Street, Barnstaple, EX31 1HP.
Tel: (01271) 322 013
Email: info@cpnd.org

The Cornelius Fund
11 Kingsley Road, Kingsbridge, TQ7 1EY.
Tel: (01548) 852 073
Email: revjohnk@supanet.com

Dorset

Bournemouth Churches Housing Association
Rent Deposit Scheme, St. Swithun's House, 21 Christchurch Road,
Bournemouth, BH1 3NS.
Tel: (01202) 410 577/560
Email: carolowen@bcha.org.uk
Website: www.bcha.org.uk

West Dorset Housing Advice
Stratton House, 58–60 High Street West, Dorchester, DT1 1UZ.
Tel: (01305) 251 010
Email: m.chamberlain@westdorset-dc.gov.uk
Website: www.westdorset-dc.gov.uk

East Sussex

Friends First
21–23 Clarendon Villas, Hove, BN3 3RE.
Tel: (01273) 747 687
Email: peter.lyndon@cck.org.uk
Website: www.cck.org.uk

Hastings & Rother Bond Board
49 Cambridge Gardens, Hastings, TN34 1EN.
Tel: (01424) 721 775
Email: mselley@bondbank.org.uk
Website: www.bondbank.org.uk

Essex

Basildon Community Resource Centre
1 The Gore, Basildon, SS14 2EA.
Tel: (01268) 450 040/1
Email: maggieviney.crc.basildon@virgin.net

Chelmsford Borough Council

Community Advice Service, Civic Centre, Coral Lane, Chelmsford, CM1 1JE.
Tel: (01245) 606 336
Email: alison.hawkins@chelmsfordbc.gov.uk

Harlow Accommodation Project

2A Wych Elm, Harlow, CM20 1QP.
Tel: (01279) 861 186
Email: harlowaccommodation@btopenworld.com

Thurrock Council

Homeless Families Unit, Civic Offices, New Road, Grays, RM17 6SL.
Tel: (01375) 652 007
Email: gogunleye@thurrock.gov.uk

Thurrock Deposit Guarantee Scheme

c/o Open Door, 24–28 Orsett Road, Grays, RM17 5EB.
Tel: (01375) 405 582
Email: opendoordgs@tiscali.co.uk

Gloucestershire

GLOFYSH Bond Scheme

4 Wellington Street, Gloucester, GL1 1RA.
Tel: (01452) 381 650
Email: glofysh@hotmail.com

South Gloucestershire Bond Scheme

23 The Parade, Coniston Road, Patchway, Bristol, BS34 5LP.
Tel: (01454) 865 742
Email: admin@sgbs.org.uk
Website: www.sgbs.org.uk

Stroud District Council

Environmental Health Services, Westward Road, Ebley, Stroud, GL5 4UB.
Tel: (01453) 754 454
Email: maria.hickman@stroud.gov.uk
Website: www.stroud.gov.uk

Tewkesbury Borough Council

Community Service, Gloucester Road, Tewkesbury, GL20 5TT.
Tel: (01684) 272 279
Email: laura.folkers@tewkesbury.gov.uk

Greater London

Brent Council Rent Deposit Guarantee Scheme
Private Housing Information Unit, Quality House, 249 Willesden Lane,
Willesden, London, NW2 5JH.
Tel: (020) 8937 2788
Email: jagdish.jethwa@brent.gov.uk
Website: www.brent.gov.uk

Equinox Rent Deposit Scheme
Unit 001, Westminster Business Square, 1–45 Durham Street, Vauxhall,
London, SE11 5JA.
Tel: (020) 7735 6521
Email: bayo@tst.equinoxcare.org.uk

London Borough of Hounslow
Rent Deposit Scheme, Housing Advice, Civic Centre, Lampton Road,
Hounslow, TW3 4DU.
Tel: (020) 8583 3848
Email: lewis.brown@hounslow.gov.uk

SmartMove (Barnet)
36B Woodhouse Road, Barnet, London, N12 0RG.
Tel: (020) 8446 3639

SmartMove (Wandsworth)
Private Rented Sector, Threshold Accommodation Project, 4th Floor,
Bedford House, 215 Balham High Road, London, SW17 7BQ.
Tel: (0208) 333 6947
Email: JSchimmefennig@thresholdhousingadvice.com

SPEAR/London Borough Richmond RDS
55 Heath Road, Twickenham, TW1 4AW.
Tel: (020) 8892 7522
Email: rds@spearlondon.org
Website: www.spearlondon.org

THATCH Help
10 Nicola Close, Harrow Weald, Harrow, HA3 5HP.
Tel: (0208) 427 4071
Email: alanpeelha3@hotmail.com

Hampshire

Rethink – Central Point Day Centre
22–24 Kingstone Road, Portsmouth, PO1 5RZ.
Tel: (023) 9229 8791
Email: mark.a.taylor@rethink.org

Southampton City Council
Deposit Guarantee Scheme, Housing Advice Centre, Southbrook Rise,
4–8 Millbrook Road East, Southampton, SO15 1YG.
Tel: (023) 8083 2977/2300
Email: steph.collier@southampton.gov.uk

Winchester Rent Deposit Scheme
16 Colebrook Street, Winchester, SO23 9LH.
Tel: (01962) 862 681

Herefordshire

Herefordshire Council
Garrick House, Widemarsh Street, Hereford, HR4 9GU.
Tel: (01432) 260 000
Email: ldawe@herefordshire.gov.uk
Website: www.herefordshire.gov.uk

Hertfordshire

Dacorum Borough Council
HAC, The Civic Centre, Hemel Hempstead, HP1 1HH.
Tel: (01442) 228 914
Email: morgan.steel@dacorum.gov.uk
Website: www.dacorum.gov.uk

Dacorum Rent Aid Rent Guarantee Scheme
Old Hempstead House, 10–12 Queensway, Hemel Hempstead,
HP1 1LR.
Tel: (01442) 251 213
Email: dacorum.rentaid@btopenworld.com
Website: www.dens.org.uk

Herts Young Homeless Group South Project
112–114 The Parade, Watford, WD17 1AU.
Tel: (01923) 231 528

Email: tina.brown@hyhg.org
Website: www.hyhg.org

St Albans District Council
Civic Centre, St Peters Street, St Albans, AL1 3JE.
Tel: (01727) 819 597
Email: C.Thomas@stalbans.gov.uk
Website: www.stalbans.gov.uk

Three Rivers District Council
Housing Needs & Resources, Three Rivers House, Northway,
Rickmansworth, WD3 1RL.
Tel: (01923) 727 061
Email: rachael.goates@threerivers.gov.uk
Website: www.threerivers.gov.uk

Kent

Ashford Borough Council
Housing Advice, The Gateway, 14 Park Mall, Ashford, TN24 8RY.
Tel: (01233) 330 374

Dover District Council
White Cliffs Business Park, Dover, CT16 3PQ.
Tel: (01304) 872 265
Email: zita.everitt@dover.gov.uk

Maidstone Borough Council
Rent Deposit Bond Scheme, London House, 5–11 London Road,
Maidstone, ME16 8HR.
Tel: (01622) 602 274
Email: vickyrogers@maidstone.gov.uk

Sevenoaks District Council
Private Sector Lettings Scheme, PO Box 1182, Argyle Road, Sevenoaks,
TN13 1GP.
Tel: (01732) 227 000
Email: Jane.Ellis@sevenoaks.gov.uk
Website: www.sevenoaks.gov.uk

SmartMove (Canterbury)
Canterbury Housing Advice Centre, 2nd Floor, 24 Burgate, Canterbury,
CT1 2HA.

Tel: (01227) 762 605
Email: canthac@aol.com

Tunbridge Wells Borough Council
Town Hall, Royal Tunbridge Wells, TN1 1RS.
Tel: (01892) 526 121

Norfolk

SmartMove (Great Yarmouth)
Herring Housing Trust, Bauleah House, 51 St Nicholas Road, Great
Yarmouth, NR30 1NR.
Tel: (01493) 331 524
Email: smartmove.gy@virgin.net

SmartMove (Kings Lynn)
The Purfleet Trust, The Granaries, Nelson Street, Kings Lynn, PE30 5RY.
Tel: (01553) 767 829
Email: aileenpurfleet@fsmail.net

South Norfolk Council
South Norfolk RADS, Strategic Housing, Long Station, Norwich,
NR15 2XE.
Tel: (01508) 533 716
Email: jbrinkley@s-norfolk.gov.uk

Oxfordshire

Banbury Homes
Rent Deposit Scheme, 1 Mawle Court, 58 George Street, Banbury,
OX16 5BH.
Tel: (01295) 676 926
Email: nab@shaftesburyhousing.org.uk
Website: www.shaftesburyhousing.org.uk

Home Choice, Housing Options
St Aldgate's Chambers, St Aldgate's, Oxford, OX1 1DF.
Tel: (01865) 252 398

Lord Mayor's Deposit Guarantee Scheme
St Aldgate's Chambers, St Aldgate's, Oxford, OX1 1EN.
Tel: (01865) 252 028

South Oxfordshire District Council
Private Sector Housing, Benson Lane, Crowmarsh Gifford, Wallingford, OX10 8BF.
Tel: (01491) 823 238
Email: elicia.bolam@southoxon.gov.uk
Website: www.southoxon.gov.uk

Somerset

Bath & District Deposit Bond Scheme
Leigh House, 1 Wells Hill, Radstock, Bath, BA3 3RN.
Tel: (01761) 432 445
Email: swan-housing@dial.pipex.com

Mendip District Council/Mendip YMCA
Rent Guarantee Scheme, The Old Glasshouse, South Street, Wells, BA5 1SL.
Tel: (01749) 670 761

Woodspring Deposit Guarantee Board
Room 9, YMCA, 2 Bristol Road Lower, Weston Super Mare, BS23 2PN.
Tel: (01934) 617 617
Email: WDGB@aol.com

Surrey

Elmbridge Rentstart
Harry Fletcher House, High Street, Esher, KT10 9RN.
Tel: (01372) 477 167
Email: elmbridge_rentstart@yahoo.co.uk

Guildford Council
Homes 4 U, Housing Advice Centre, Millmead House, Millmead, Guildford, GU2 4BB.
Tel: (01483) 444 267
Email: eatonc@guildford.gov.uk

Kingston Churches Action on Homelessness
The Access Project, 36A Fife Road, Kingston Upon Thames, KT1 1SU.
Tel: (020) 8255 2439
Email: kcah@dial.pipex.com
Website: www.kcah.org.uk

Reigate & Redhill YMCA
Next Step Rent Deposit Scheme, Hillbrook House, 68 Brighton Road, Redhill, RH1 6QT.
Tel: (01737) 773 089
Email: gina.widnell@ymcaredhill.com

Runnymede Borough Council
Private Sector Resettlement Team, Civic Offices, Station Road, Addlestone, KT15 1AH.
Tel: (01932) 425 874/815
Website: www.runnymede.gov.uk

Runnymede Rentstart
12–13 The Sainsbury Centre, Chertsey, KT16 9AG.
Tel: (01932) 567 621
Email: rentstart@ukf.net

Tandridge Rent Deposit Scheme
The Star Centre, Oxted Library, Oxted, RH8 0BQ.
Tel: (01883) 715 785
Email: tvsc@btconnect.com

Waverley Borough Council Rent Deposit Scheme
Council Offices, The Burys, Godalming, GU7 1HR.
Tel: (01483) 523 360
Email: sbryden@waverley.gov.uk
Website: www.waverley.gov.uk

Woking Churches Rent Guarantee Scheme
The Crescent Project, Heathside Crescent, Woking, GU21 7AJ.
Tel: (01483) 772 265
Email: wcrgs@scdt.org.uk

Warwickshire

Nuneaton & Bedworth Doorway Deposit Scheme
20 High Street, Bedworth, CV12 8NF.
Tel: (0247) 674 0400
Email: doorway@doorway.fsnet.co.uk
Website: www.doorway.fsnet.co.uk

West Sussex

Crawley Rent Start Scheme
Crawley Borough Council, Housing Strategic Services, Town Hall, The Boulevard, Crawley, RH10 1UZ.
Tel: (01293) 438 445

Littlehampton Churches Together Homelink
The Bradbury Centre, 1–5 St Martin's Lane, Littlehampton, BN17 6BS.
Tel: (01903) 739 669
Email: lct.homelink@talk21.com

Worcestershire

Bromsgrove Youth Homeless Forum
The Basement, New Road, Bromsgrove, B60 2JD.
Tel: (01527) 832 993
Email: elaine@bromsgroveyouth.fsnet.co.uk

Elgar Housing Association
Grovewood Road, Malvern Link, WR14 1GD.
Tel: (01684) 579 579
Email: cmckelvie@festivalhousing.org

SmartMove (Worcester)
Worcester Housing & Benefits Advice Centre, 13A Lowesmoor, Worcester, WR1 2RS.
Tel: (0190) 520 055
Email: enquiries@whabac.org.uk
Website: www.whabac.org.uk

The Step Up Private Tenancy Scheme
Bromsgrove and District Citizens Advice Bureau, 50–52 Birmingham Road, Bromsgrove, B61 0DD.
Tel: (01527) 557 397

Wychavon District Council
Civic Centre, Queen Elizabeth Drive, Pershore, WR10 1PT.
Tel: (01386) 565 484
Email: kath.smith@wychavon.gov.uk
Website: www.wychavon.gov.uk

Northern Ireland

Co Down

Simon Community
Rent Deposit Scheme, 259 Antrim Road, Belfast, BT7 1HT.
Tel: (028) 9075 6971

SmartMove (Belfast)
193 Antrim Road, Belfast, BT15 2GW.
Tel: (028) 9075 7801
Email: smartmove.belfast@btopenworld.com

Co. Tyrone

Council for the Homeless Northern Ireland
72 North Street, Belfast, BT1 1LD.
Tel: (028) 9024 6440
Email: info@chni.org.uk
Website: www.chni.org.uk

Derry

SmartMove (Derry)
28A Bishop Street, Derry, BT48 6PP.
Tel: (028) 7136 3256

Scotland

Argyll & Bute

Argyll & Bute Rent Deposit Scheme
1st Floor, WHHA Building, Crannog Lane, Oban, PA34 4HB.
Tel: (01631) 572 183
Email: douglas.whyte@argyll-bute.gov.uk

Dumfries and Galloway

Nithsdale Council of Voluntary Service
Rent Deposit Guarantee Scheme, Holywood Building, Old Assembly
Close, Irish Street, Dumfries, DG1 2PH.

Tel: (01387) 269 161
Email: karenlewis@ncvs.org.uk

East Ayrshire

Community Housing Advocacy Project

Marlin House, 12 Heatherhouse Road, Irvine, KA12 8HQ.
Tel: (01294) 313 137
Email: scarson@chap.org.uk
Website: www.chap.org.uk

East Dunbartonshire

East Dunbartonshire Council

c/o Homeless Team (EDC), Enterprise House, Southbank Business Park,
Kirkintilloch, Glasgow, G66 1XQ.
Tel: (0141) 578 2161
Email: sheila.fitzpatrick@eastdunbarton.gov.uk
Website: www.eastdunbarton.gov.uk

East Renfrewshire

East Renfrewshire CAB

216 Main Street, Barrhead, G78 1SN.
Tel: (0141) 881 3660
Email: jeanettemcgale@eastrenfrewshirecab.casonline.org.uk

Edinburgh

Smartmove (Edinburgh)

Edinburgh Cyrenians, Norton Park, 57 Albion Road, Edinburgh,
EH7 5QY.
Tel: (0131) 475 2356
Email: becky@cyrenians.org.uk
Website: www.cyrenians.org.uk

Falkirk

Falkirk Homeless Project

Falkirk Rent Deposit Guarantee Scheme, Unit 6, LEC Court, Bog
Industrial Estate, Laurieston, FK2 9PH.

Tel: (01324) 622 900
Email: falkirkRDGS@aol.com

Fife

Fife Keyfund
Cairn Centre, 83–85 Dunnikier Road, Kirkcaldy, KY1 2QW.
Tel: (01592) 201 849
Email: fifekeyfund@aol.com

Glasgow

Glasgow Rent Deposit and Support Scheme
Crowngate Business Centre, Brook Street, Glasgow, G40 3AP.
Tel: (0141) 550 7140
Email: mail@grdss.org
Website: www.grdss.org

Inverclyde

Inverclyde Council
Homeless Services, Inverclyde Centre, 98 Dalrymple Street, Greenock,
PA15 1BZ.
Tel: (01475) 715 879
Email: roslyn.mclaughlin@inverclyde.gov.uk

Moray

Moray Council – Keyfund
Housing Services, 12–14 Grey Friars Street, Elgin, IV30 1LF.
Tel: (01343) 563 591
Website: www.moray.gov.uk

North Ayrshire

North Ayrshire Council
Rent Deposit Guarantee Scheme, Cunninghame House, Irvine,
KA12 8EE.
Tel: (01294) 475 452
Email: mlivingstone@north-ayrshire.gov.uk

Orkney Islands

Advice and Information Section
Housing Division, Orkney Islands Council, School Place, Kirkwall, KW15 1NY.
Tel: (01856) 873 535
Email: housingadvice@orkney.gov.uk
Website: www.orkney.gov.uk

Perth & Kinross

CATH Keyfund
5 Back Wynd, Bridgend, Perth, PH2 7DX.
Tel: (01738) 783 249
Email: j.guthrie@cath-org.co.uk

Renfrewshire

Renfrewshire Deposit Guarantee Scheme
Renfrewshire CAB, 45 George Street, Paisley, PA1 2JY.
Tel: (0141) 889 4789
Email: janemurphy@PaisleyCAB.casonline.org.uk

South Ayrshire

SEASCAPE
13 Old Bridge Street, Ayr, KA7 1QA.
Tel: (01292) 285 424
Email: margaretmcdowall@seascapeayr.co.uk

South Lanarkshire

South Lanarkshire Rent Deposit Scheme
10–14 Duke Street, Hamilton, ML3 7DT.
Tel: (01698) 891 551
Email: slrsi@ymcaglasgow.org

Stirling

Stirling Rent Deposit Guarantee Scheme
49 St John Street, Stirling, FK8 1ED.
Tel: (01786) 472 247
Email: bill@cowanes.org.uk; macdonald@stirling.gov.uk

West Lothian

Edinburgh Cyrenians – West Lothian RDGS
Unit Q, Kirkton Business Centre, Kirk Lane, Livingston, EH54 7AY.
Tel: (01506) 205 413

Western Isles

First Base
Housing Department, Comhairle nan Eilean Siar, Sandwick Road,
Stornoway, HS1 2BW.
Tel: (01851) 709 374
Email: l.graham@cne-siar.gov.uk

Wales

Bridgend

SmartMove (Bridgend)
Bridgend Bond Board, 5A Market Street, Bridgend, CF31 1LL.
Tel: (01656) 654 442
Website: www.wallichclifford.com

Cardiff

Cardiff Bond Board
Marland House, Central Square, Cardiff, CF10 1EP.
Tel: (029) 2087 1333
Email: cbb@cardiff-bond-board.org.uk
Website: www.cardiff-bond-board.org.uk

YMCA (Wales) Rent Deposit Scheme
3rd Floor, 33 Westgate Street, Cardiff, CF10 1JE.
Tel: (029) 2078 5028

Carmarthenshire

Carmarthenshire Bond Scheme
107 Station Road, Llanelli, SA15 1YS.
Tel: (01554) 740 012
Email: carms.bond@gwalia.com

Ceredigion

Bond Ceredigion
Ceredigion Care Society, 1 North Parade, Aberystwyth, SY23 2JH.
Tel: (01970) 639 111
Email: ceredigioncare@btconnect.com

Conwy

Conwy & Denbighshire Bond Scheme
2nd Floor Offices, Aberconwy House, 1 Trinity Square, Llandudno,
LL30 1PY.
Tel: (01492) 860 437
Email: dewi.wood@nacro.org.uk
Website: www.nacro.org.uk

Flintshire

B&B Spend to Save Pilot Scheme (Family Bond Scheme)
County Offices, Chapel Street, Flint, CF6 5PD.
Tel: (01352) 703 808
Email: kay_burgess@flintshire.gov.uk

Flintshire County Council
YMCA Wales, County Offices, Flint, CH6 5PD.
Tel: (01352) 703 811
Email: ann_lockett@flintshire.gov.uk

Landlord/Landlady Scheme
County Offices, Chapel Street, Flint, CH6 5PD.
Tel: (01352) 703 808
Email: kay_burgess@flintshire.gov.uk

Glamorgan

Dewis
47 Station Road, Port Talbot, SA13 1NW.
Tel: (01639) 882 536
Email: mail@dewishousing.org

Neath Port Talbot County Borough Council
Neath Civic Centre, Neath, SA11 3QZ.

Tel: (01639) 764 456
Email: s.foley2@npt.gov.uk

Gwent

Move on Project
119 Commercial Street, Risca, Newport, NP12 6AZ.
Tel: (01633) 613 405

Gwynedd

Agorfa Bond Scheme
Mount House, 4 Mount Street, Bangor, LL57 1BQ.
Tel: (01248) 355 058
Email: wil.williams@agorfa.org
Website: www.agorfa.org

Monmouthshire

Monmouthshire Bond Scheme
20 The Woodlands, Mamhilad Park Estate, Pontypool, NP4 0HZ.
Tel: (01495) 764 156

Newport

RightMove (The Newport Bond Scheme)
Rehousing Services Office, The Bus Station, Kingsway, Newport, NP20 1EY.
Tel: (01633) 232 594
Email: vicky.davies@newport.gov.uk

Pembrokeshire

Pembrokeshire Care Society
20 Upper Market Street, Haverfordwest, SA61 1QA.
Tel: (01437) 765 335
Email: pemcare@btconnect.com
Website: www.pembrokeshirecaresociety.co.uk

Powys

Powys Deposit Guarantee Scheme
Flat 1, Fairview, Temple Street, Llandrindod Wells, LD1 5HF.

Tel: (01597) 825 855
Email: jane.hill@gwalia.com

Rhondda Cynon

Rhondda Cynon Taff Bond Board
Housing Advice Centre, 10–12 Gelliwastad Road, Pontypridd, CF37 2BW.
Tel: (01443) 485 515

Swansea

National Council of YMCAs (Wales)
Partnerships Manager, Metropole Chambers, Salubrious Passage,
Swansea, SA1 3RT.
Tel: (029) 2078 5028
Email: mandy.smithson@south-wales.probation.gsx.gov.uk

Swansea Bond Board
Wallich Clifford Community, 49 Walter Road, Swansea, SA1 5PW.
Tel: (01792) 301 363
Email: swanseabondboard@wallichclifford.net
Website: www.wallichclifford.com

Torfaen

Right Move
Monmouthshire County Council, Housing Department, County Hall,
Cwmbran, NP44 2XH.
Tel: (01633) 644 472
Email: michelemorgan@monmouthshire.gov.uk

Vale of Glamorgan

Home Access
Tabernacle Baptist Church, Plassey Street, Penarth, CF64 1EN.
Tel: (029) 2070 2690
Email: homeaccess96@yahoo.co.uk

SmartMove (Vale of Glamorgan)
Llamau Limited, JIGSO, 240 Holton Road, Barry, CF63 4HS.
Tel: (01446) 748 852
Email: sa@llamauvale.freeserve.co.uk

List of hotspots

What is a hotspot?

First of all, we need to define a hotspot. A hotspot is an area where there are properties available for sale that fall into one of these three categories:

Gold – Property prices are predicted to rise at a greater rate than the national average and the rental yield is greater than the national average.

Silver – The rental yield is greater than the national average.

Bronze – Property prices are predicted to rise at a greater rate than the national average.

I've ranked the categories with Gold being the most desirable as Gold enjoys the best of both worlds – capital growth and yield thus spreading the return and overall risk. Silver is ranked second as the yield is a certain outcome, whereas the capital growth for Bronze is uncertain.

I've found, in my experience, that investors choose categories Gold, Silver or Bronze on personal circumstances, but they rely more so on gut reaction. My advice is to choose all of them! There is no need to place all your eggs in one basket. Property is a relatively safe investment, but there is a degree of uncertainty, so, if possible, by investing in all the categories above, you should eliminate some of the business risk.

Identification of a hotspot

So how did I identify the hotspots listed? Well the categories are based on two factors:

1. Actual rental yields
2. Predicted property prices

Actual rental yields

The first factor, actual rental yields, was easy to do. Actual rental yield is:

$$\frac{\text{actual yearly rent}}{\text{actual property price}}$$

Since these figures are actuals, I collated all the rental figures from local letting agents in the UK, all the local property prices in the UK from the Land Registry, and calculated all the yields being offered from all UK locations. I then eliminated all the poor yielding locations where I thought tenant demand was low (even if they were high yielding).

Predicted property prices

Here I didn't predict the property prices as this is an impossible thing to do. If I could, I wouldn't be writing this book but buying everything I could in a hotspot area! All I did was look at what would make an area's property price rise above the national average. I came up with the following:

1. Proposed transportation link improvements, such as improved road and rail links, expansion of local airports and improved public transport.

2. Proposed inward investment from private companies, the government and trusts.

3. Proposed improvements to leisure facilities, such as sport centres, parks and shopping centres.

4. The likelihood of holiday seasons being lengthened for holiday areas.

5. My own experience gathered from being in this industry and from comments from letting and estate agents.

My top 10

All these areas are category Gold and are listed in alphabetical order.

Area:	Bethnal Green, London, E2
Demand for letting:	Excellent
Average void period:	7 days

Description:

I find this place amazing. It's only a £6 cab ride or a three-minute tube journey from the heart of the financial capital of the world! Yet the area looks run down in places, with only a few pockets being 'nice' areas. The nice areas being the old ex-local authority Victorian flats, such as on Corfield Street, off Bethnal Green Road (which are no more than five storeys high), ubiquitous developers' loft conversions of disused schools and warehouses into flats, and new builds such as Millennium Place, opposite Cambridge Heath Station.

These areas are highly sought-after by young professionals who work in the City. I think that these young professionals don't mind taking the risk in living in these East End ex-gangster-type areas, as they get a lot more for their money. Shoreditch is only a brief stroll down Bethnal Green Road and there they enter into the trendy-bar city where other young professional 20-somethings meet up.

Tenant demand will be strong if the financial economy is flourishing as this area relies on jobs being provided by the City, but be aware that the state of the financial economy can change quite rapidly. We're heavily linked to the US economy so it pays to keep abreast of what's going on across the Atlantic.

Queen Mary's Hospital & College is a five-minute walk and hence the area proves to be popular with medical students. The college is keen to hear from landlords, as there is a shortage of student accommodation and it offers a fee-free tenant finding service.

I think out of all the areas in London this area will be the most different in 20 years to what it is today. It's ripe for gentrification and close enough to the burgeoning financial hub to be gobbled up and turned into a support centre of hotels, restaurants and bars for international business visitors.

Tube:	Bethnal Green. Central Line – Zone 2. Three minutes to Liverpool Street.

Area:	**Corby, Northamptonshire, NN18**
Demand for letting:	Excellent
Average void period:	5 days

Description:

Corby was home to the big steel and iron industries, which employed a significant proportion of the population, but they closed down in the 1980s. This resulted in high unemployment initially, but it has partly recovered with the arrival of a number of smaller manufacturing and distribution industries.

I have 20 properties in this area. Due to the above average unemployment, a lot of my properties are let to DSS claimants. Corby is a new town so there are plenty of ex-local authority flats and homes for sale in order to meet this demand.

My experience with the council is a mixed one – sometimes they process the benefit applications efficiently and sometimes not. In the past, I've had to wait for payments to come through for up to 20 weeks, but the council has since improved.

Tenant demand is strong. If I put an advert in the local press, I'll get at least 10 calls and the property will be let within the week. There is a high Scottish population and many who wish to move to England come to Corby first.

Mainline railway station:	None. Corby bus station to Peterborough train station. Peterborough is one hour to London.
Road access:	A14. 90 miles to London and 60 miles to Birmingham.
Local newspaper:	Northants Evening Telegraph – Tel: (01536) 506 100

Area:	**Derby, Derbyshire, DE1**
Demand for letting:	Good
Average void period:	8 days

Description:

The decision by Toyota to invest £1.15bn in its European production facility close to Derby has seen further investment in the transport manufacturing sector. Output levels from the Burnaston factory have reached 282,000 cars a year and Toyota now employs over 4,250 people at Burnaston. This has sustained demand for rental properties in Derby and it will continue to do so.

The city has a diverse and active economy with a level of performance equal to any other in the East Midlands. Derby has seen its traditional employment base shift towards the service sector over the past decade – an example being the recent call centre investment by Prudential Banking plc (Egg).

Its central location is highly desirable for distribution purposes as it has access to all the key markets in the UK.

Mainline railway station:	Derby. One hour 49 minutes to London.
Road access:	M1. 130 miles to Greater London.
Local newspaper:	Derby Evening Telegraph – Tel: (01332) 292 929

Area:	Grimsby, Lincolnshire, DN31
Demand for letting:	Good
Average void period:	10 days
Description:	

Once famous for its fishing industry, Grimsby has carved a new identity in recent years as a centre for food processing, pharmaceuticals and petrochemicals. It's also famous for coming top in Dun & Bradstreet's survey, which showed that 88.5% of Grimsby's businesses are profitable – the highest in the country.

Unemployment is higher than the national average, so this area will appeal to the investor who doesn't mind having DSS claimants as tenants.

The area is well connected. It's less than three hours to London by rail and is only a four-minute drive to Humberside Airport. The Humber Bridge can get you to the ferry port in Hull in less than an hour and it's a gateway to the area.

Mainline railway station:	Grimsby Town. Two hours to York.
Road access:	Main access A16 and A46. 36 miles north east of Lincoln. 21 miles from M180.
Local newspaper:	Grimsby Evening Telegraph – Tel: (01472) 360 360

Area:	**Huddersfield, Yorkshire, HD1**
Demand for letting:	Good
Average void period:	9 days
Description:	

Over the next 10 years, the total population of Kirklees is forecast to have the highest growth rate in West Yorkshire. Huddersfield University is anticipating an increase in the number of students over the decade, which will have a positive impact on the local service sector and on housing demand.

Huddersfield is a commuter area for people working in Leeds. Property prices in Leeds are significantly higher than Huddersfield so the possibility for capital growth is high due to workers in Leeds being priced out.

There is a readily available stock of housing in Huddersfield so if you're looking to build a portfolio quickly, you'll have no problem here.

Unemployment is higher than the national average, so the DSS market is large.

Mainline railway station:	Huddersfield. 34 minutes to Manchester and 2 hours 50 minutes to London.
Road access:	M62. 29 miles to Manchester and 222 miles to London.
Local newspaper:	Huddersfield Examiner – Tel: (01484) 430 000

Area:	**Mansfield, Nottingham, NG18**
Demand for letting:	Good
Average void period:	14 days
Description:	

This area provides excellent value for any property investor. There is a ready supply of terraced houses to purchase with good yields. This area is ripe for capital growth and is next on my list of places for me to invest personally.

Unemployment is above average so demand will exist from DSS benefit applicants.

Mainline railway station:	Mansfield. Two hours 30 minutes to London.
Road access:	M1. 141 miles to London and 59 miles to Leeds.
Local newspaper:	Mansfield & Ashfield Recorder – Tel: (01623) 420 000 Mansfield & Ashfield Observer – Tel: (01623) 465 555 Mansfield CHAD – Tel: (01623) 464 749

Area:	**Neath Port Talbot, Glamorgan, South Wales, SA11**
Demand for letting:	OK
Average void period:	11 days
Description:	

Neath has higher than average wages with lower than average property prices, hence the area could afford an increase in property prices.

Neath's economy today is much more diversified with light industry replacing the heavy industrial sector. New inward investment has been secured from both the UK and overseas and growth has been achieved through infrastructure developments and innovative approaches to business support services.

Corus (formally British Steel) remains the largest industrial employer in the county borough and a major contributor to the local economy.

The tourism industry contributes significantly to the local economy, attracting over 1.4m people to its main tourist attractions and bringing an estimated £23m into the local authority.

The service sector is becoming increasingly important to the local economy, and the opportunity for growth in this sector is good, with a number of good quality sites already established and further developments proposed.

Mainline railway station:	Neath. 45 minutes to Cardiff.
Road access:	M4. 189 miles to London and 41 miles to Cardiff.
Local newspaper:	South Wales Evening Post – Tel: (01792) 514 000 Port Talbot Guardian – Tel: (01639) 778 888

Area:	**Salford, Manchester, M6**
Demand for letting:	OK
Average void period:	18 days
Description:	

Salford's location in the heart of Greater Manchester provides access to a large domestic market of over 2.5m. Salford's economy is an open one. A considerable proportion of Salford's population continues to work outside the city, particularly in the Regional Centre and Trafford Park.

The unemployment rate is below average for the UK.

The city is developing its Innovation Park and this is expected to support companies including inward investors and a growing number of spinouts from the university.

The yields are fantastic. Hence competition is fierce, so expect longer void periods.

Mainline railway station:	Salford Central. Three hours 21 minutes to London.
Road access:	M602. 215 miles to London and 93 miles to Birmingham.
Local newspaper:	Salford Advertiser – Tel: (0161) 789 5015

Area:	**Stockton-on-Tees, Cleveland, TS18**
Demand for letting:	Good
Average void period:	10 days

Description:

I think that there will be above average property price growth in this area which will compensate for the sub-12% yields. There has been major inward investment for the creation of several commercial sites including Teesdale, Belasis Hall Technology Park and Chemplex. This can only mean strong demand for rental properties for people on short- to medium-term contracts.

The riverside town centre is thriving with more than 30 medium-to-large enterprises including manufacturing, retail, office and storage facilities.

There is plenty of demand from the university sector, if you wish to enter this market, from the University of Teeside and the Stockton campus for the University of Durham. It's worth contacting the universities as they offer a free service to landlords placing students in private rented properties.

Mainline railway station:	Stockton. Three hours 42 minutes to London.
Road access:	A19 and A66. 275 miles to London. 66 miles to Leeds.
Local newspaper:	East Cleveland Herald & Post – Tel: (01642) 252 525

Area:	**Stoke-on-Trent, Staffordshire, ST6**
Demand for letting:	Good
Average void period:	12 days

Description:

This city has six major towns in the area – Burslem, Fenton, Hanley, Longton, Stoke and Tunstall. All these areas offer cheap and affordable investment properties with decent yields.

The city is in the heart of the ceramics industry and includes the headquarters and manufacturing bases of most of the UK's leading pottery companies. It's also home to centres of excellence, such as the British Ceramic Confederation, CERAM Research and the Hothouse Centre for Ceramic Design. This concentration of manufacturers and support organisations provides the basis for the local economy. 4m people visit the city every year because of the potteries and this provides over 5,000 jobs for the local economy.

Plenty of new jobs have been created recently in the service sector – mainly call centres and logistics reflecting the city's large catchment area workforce and road links. Unemployment is slightly above average, but I don't think that this has a significant effect on the local economy.

Stoke-on-Trent is a city undergoing change. Its availability to cheap and skilled labour, its location and growing university are helping to create a new thriving city.

It's in the centre of the country, midway between Manchester and Birmingham and has excellent communications. New transport links have opened up prime development sites for inward commercial investors. Significant new investment has seen the city centre firmly established as the shopping and cultural centre for the region. Leading high street names are found in and around the award winning Potteries Centre, and major show and events are hosted in the city's theatres.

Mainline railway station:	Stoke-on-Trent. One hour 50 minutes to London, one hour to Birmingham and 50 minutes to Manchester.
Local newspaper:	The Sentinel – Tel: (01782) 602 525

The rest of the hotspots listed below are Silver and Bronze. As a rule of thumb, London and the Home Counties are Bronze and the rest are Silver.

England East Anglia

1. Attleborough, Norfolk
2. Boston, Lincolnshire
3. Brookenby, Lincolnshire
4. Bungay, Norfolk
5. Chatteris, Cambridgeshire
6. Cromer, Norfolk
7. Downham Market, Norfolk
8. Eye, Suffolk
9. Grantham, Lincolnshire
10. Hadleigh, Suffolk

11.   Ipswich, Suffolk
12.   Kings Lynn, Norfolk
13.   Lincoln, Lincolnshire
14.   Market Rasen, Lincolnshire
15.   Mundesley, Norfolk
16.   Norwich, Norfolk
17.   Orton Goldhay, Peterborough, Cambridgeshire
18.   Orton Malbourne, Peterborough, Cambridgeshire
19.   St Neots, Cambridgeshire
20.   Skegness, Lincolnshire
21.   Sudbury, Suffolk
22.   Welland, Peterborough, Cambridgeshire
23.   Wickham Market, Woodbridge, Suffolk
24.   Wisbech, Cambridgeshire

England Essex, Herts and Middlesex

1.   Aveley, Essex
2.   Basildon, Essex
3.   Clacton-on-Sea, Essex
4.   Colchester, Essex
5.   Dagenham, Essex
6.   East Tilbury, Essex
7.   Enfield, Middlesex
8.   Frinton-on-Sea, Essex
9.   Grays, Essex
10.   Halstead, Essex
11.   Harlow, Essex
12.   Harold Hill, Essex
13.   Harwich, Essex
14.   Hornchurch, Essex
15.   Laindon, Essex
16.   Pitsea, Essex
17.   Purfleet, Essex
18.   Rainham, Essex
19.   Romford, Essex
20.   Sawbridgeworth, Herts
21.   Sheerness, Essex
22.   Shoeburyness, Essex

23. South Ockendon, Essex
24. Southend, Essex
25. Stanford Le Hope, Essex
26. Tilbury, Essex
27. Waltham Cross, Herts
28. Westcliffe-on-Sea, Essex
29. Wickford, Essex
30. Witham, Essex

England London

1. Beckton
2. Bexley Heath
3. Leyton
4. Northolt
5. Plaistow
6. Streatham
7. Thamesmead
8. Walthamstow
9. West Hendon
10. Woolwich

England Mid North

1. Balby, Doncaster, Yorkshire
2. Beeston, Leeds
3. Castleford, Yorkshire
4. Crossgates, Leeds
5. Dewsbury, Yorkshire
6. Garforth, Yorkshire
7. Goole, Yorkshire
8. Hull, Yorkshire
9. Marsden, Yorkshire
10. Pocklington, Yorkshire
11. Rochdale, Lancashire
12. Rotherham, Yorkshire
13. Roundhay, Yorkshire
14. Scarborough, Yorkshire
15. Scunthorpe, Lincolnshire
16. Skipton, Bradford, Yorkshire

17. Wakefield, Yorkshire

England Midlands

1. Anstey Heights, Leicestershire
2. Aspley, Notts
3. Bedford, Bedfordshire
4. Bestwood, Notts
5. Bilborough, Notts
6. Binley, Coventry, Warwickshire
7. Bobbersmill, Notts
8. Braunstone, Leicester, Leicestershire
9. Broxtowe, Notts
10. Bulwell, Notts
11. Burton-on-Trent, Staffordshire
12. Camphill, Northants
13. Clifton, Notts
14. Daventry, Warwickshire
15. Dudley, West Midlands
16. Dunstable, Bedfordshire
17. Foleshill, Coventry, Warwickshire
18. Highbury Vale, Notts
19. Hodge Hill, Birmingham, West Midlands
20. Ilkeston, Notts
21. Irthlingborough, Northants
22. Kettering, Northants
23. Kimberley, Notts
24. Kirkby-in-Ashfield, Notts
25. Leicester City Centre, Leicestershire
26. Luton, Bedfordshire
27. Moulton, Northants
28. Newark, Notts
29. Newcastle-under-Lyme, Staffordshire
30. Newstead Village, Hucknall, Notts
31. Northampton, Northants
32. Oldbury, West Midlands
33. Rednal, Birmingham, West Midlands
34. Rugby, Warwickshire
35. Rushden, Northants

36. Shrewsbury, Shropshire
37. Strelley, Notts
38. Sutton-in-Ashfield, Notts
39. The Meadows, Notts
40. Thorneywood, Notts
41. Thorpelands, Northants
42. Top Valley, Notts
43. Walsall, West Midlands
44. Warren Hill, Notts
45. Wellingborough, Northants
46. Willenhall, Coventry
47. Wolverhampton, West Midlands

England North East

1. Arthurs Hill, Newcastle, Tyne & Wear
2. Benwell, Newcastle, Tyne & Wear
3. Bishop Auckland, Darlington, Durham
4. Blakelaw, West Denton, Tyne & Wear
5. Blyth, Newcastle, Tyne & Wear
6. Carlisle, Northumberland
7. Chilton, Darlington, Durham
8. Colliery, Durham
9. Consett, Durham
10. Elswick, Tyne & Wear
11. Ferryhill, Spennymoor, Durham
12. Gateshead, Newcastle, Tyne & Wear
13. Hartlepool, Durham
14. Hebburn, Tyne & Wear
15. Hendon, Sunderland, Tyne & Wear
16. Hexham, Northumberland
17. Houghton-le-Spring, Tyne & Wear
18. Lemington, West Denton, Tyne & Wear
19. Middlesbrough, Cleveland
20. Newcastle-upon-Tyne, Tyne & Wear
21. Newton Aycliffe, Darlington
22. Prudhoe, Northumberland
23. Redcar, Cleveland
24. Ryton, Crawcrook, Gateshead

25. Seaham, Durham
26. South Shields, Newcastle, Tyne & Wear
27. Walkergate, Tyne & Wear
28. Wallsend, Newcastle, Tyne & Wear
29. Washington, Tyne & Wear

England North West

1. Accrington, Lancashire
2. Allerton, Liverpool
3. Bacup, Manchester
4. Barnsley, Lancashire
5. Birkenhead, Lancashire
6. Blackburn, Lancashire
7. Blackpool, Lancashire
8. Bolton, Manchester
9. Bootle, Liverpool
10. Bradford, Yorkshire
11. Broughton, Cheshire
12. Bury, Lancashire
13. Chester, Cheshire
14. Clayton, Manchester
15. Colne, Lancashire
16. Crewe, Cheshire
17. Darwen, Lancashire
18. Denton, Manchester
19. Eccles, Manchester
20. Eddington, Doncaster, Yorkshire
21. Farnworth, Lancashire
22. Gainsborough, Manchester
23. Golborne, Cheshire
24. Halifax, Yorkshire
25. Holywell, Flintshire
26. Huyton, Prescot, Liverpool
27. Hyde Park, Manchester
28. Keighley, Yorkshire
29. Kirkby, Maghull, Merseyside
30. Leigh, Lancashire
31. Liverpool, L4

32. Liverpool, L6
33. Liverpool, L7
34. Liverpool, L8
35. Liverpool, L9
36. Liverpool, L13
37. Liverpool, L14
38. Liverpool, L20
39. Longsight, Manchester
40. Mexborough, Yorkshire
41. Morecambe, Lancashire
42. Moss Side, Manchester
43. Northwich, Cheshire
44. Openshaw, Manchester
45. Peasley Cross, Merseyside
46. Preston, Lancashire
47. Rishton, Lancashire
48. Rock Ferry, Bebington, Cheshire
49. Rotherham, Yorkshire
50. Runcorn, Cheshire
51. Rusholme, Manchester
52. St Helens, Merseyside
53. Sheffield City Centre, Yorkshire
54. Swinton, Manchester
55. Wallasey, Merseyside
56. Walton Vale, Lancashire
57. Warrington, Lancashire
58. Waterloo, Lancashire
59. West Derby, Merseyside
60. Wigan, Manchester
61. Winsford, Cheshire
62. Withlington, Manchester
63. Wombwell, Yorkshire
64. Worksop, Manchester
65. Worsley, Manchester

England South

1. Bexhill-on-Sea, Sussex
2. Bognor Regis, Sussex

3. Bournemouth, Dorset
4. Fareham, Hampshire
5. Rottingdean, Brighton, Sussex
6. Rowner, Gosport, Hampshire
7. Ryde, Isle of Wight
8. St Leonards-on-Sea, Sussex
9. St Marys, Southampton, Hampshire
10. Sandown, Isle of Wight
11. Shirley, Southampton, Hampshire
12. Sholing, Southampton, Hampshire
13. Southbourne, Dorset
14. Southsea, Hampshire
15. Thornhill, Southampton, Hampshire

England South East

1. Ashford, Kent
2. Broadstairs, Kent
3. Canterbury, Kent
4. Chatham, Kent
5. Cliftonville, Kent
6. Dartford, Kent
7. Dover, Kent
8. Eastbourne, Sussex
9. Erith, Kent
10. Faversham, Kent
11. Folkstone, Kent
12. Hastings, Sussex
13. Herne Bay, Kent
14. Margate, Kent
15. Ramsgate, Kent
16. Rochester, Kent
17. Sittingbourne, Kent
18. Snodland, Kent
19. Westgate-on-Sea, Kent

England South West

1. Avon, Bristol
2. Axminster, Devon

3. Bodmin, Cornwall
4. Bovey Tracey, Devon
5. Bridgewater, Taunton, Somerset
6. Callington, Cornwall
7. Chard, Somerset
8. Chelston, Devon
9. Clevedon, Bristol
10. Dawlish, Devon
11. Devonport, Plymouth, Devon
12. Filton, Bristol
13. Gillingham, Dorset
14. Honicknowle, Plymouth, Devon
15. Hooe, Plymouth, Devon
16. Houndstone, Somerset
17. Ilfracombe, Devon
18. Ilminster, Somerset
19. Keyham, Plymouth, Devon
20. Laira, Plymouth, Devon
21. Launceston, Cornwall
22. Lipson, Plymouth, Devon
23. Looe, Plymouth, Devon
24. Paignton, Devon
25. Plymouth City Centre, Plymouth, Devon
26. St Beaudeaux, Plymouth, Devon
27. Shepton Mallet, Somerset
28. Stoke, Plymouth, Devon
29. Stratton Creber, Newquay, Cornwall
30. Tavistock, Devon
31. Teignmouth, Devon
32. Topsham, Devon
33. Torquay, Devon
34. Wellington, Somerset
35. Westbury, Bath, Somerset
36. Weston Super Mare, Somerset
37. Yeovil, Somerset

England West

1. Caldicot, Gloucs

2. Churchdown, Gloucs
3. Cinderford, Gloucs
4. Coleford, Gloucs
5. Hardwicke, Gloucs
6. Hereford, Herefordshire
7. Kidderminster, Worcestershire
8. Newtown Farm, Herefordshire
9. Redditch, Worcestershire
10. Tewkesbury, Gloucs
11. Worcester, Worcestershire

Scotland

1. Airdrie, Lanarkshire
2. Alexandria, Dumbarton, Dunbartonshire
3. Beith, Bridge of Weir, Ayrshire
4. Bellshill, Lanarkshire
5. Bridgeton, Glasgow
6. Broxburn, Livingston, West Lothian
7. Carstairs Junction, Lanarkshire
8. Chapelhall, Airdrie, Lanarkshire
9. Cleland, Lanarkshire
10. Craigshill, Livingston, West Lothian
11. Cronberry, Ayr, Ayrshire
12. Dalry, Bridge of Weir, Ayrshire
13. Darvel, Kilmarnock, Ayrshire
14. Dennistown, Glasgow
15. Dumbarton, Dunbartonshire
16. East Kilbride, Glasgow
17. Falkirk, Falkirk
18. Glengarnock, Bridge of Weir, Ayrshire
19. Glenrothes, Fife
20. Greenock, Renfrewshire
21. Govanhill, Glasgow
22. Hamilton, Lanarkshire
23. Ibrox, Glasgow
24. Inverkeithing, Dalgety Bay, Fife
25. Kilbirnie, Bridge of Weir, Ayrshire
26. Kilsyth, Glasgow

27. Kilwinning, Troon, Ayrshire
28. Kirkcaldy, Fife
29. Kirkintolloch, Bishopsbriggs, Dunbartonshire
30. Lochgelly, Fife
31. Maybole, Ayr, Ayrshire
32. New Cumnock, Ayr, Ayrshire
33. Newmilus, Kilmarnock, Ayrshire
34. North Carbrain, Lanarkshire
35. Paisley, Renfrewshire
36. Port Glasgow, Renfrewshire
37. Preisthill, Glasgow
38. Saracen Cross, Glasgow
39. Springboig, Glasgow
40. Stewarton, Kilmarnock, Ayrshire
41. Tollcross, Glasgow
42. Whitburn, Livingston, West Lothian
43. Wishaw, Lanarkshire
44. Yoker, Glasgow

Wales

1. Abercynon, Pontypridd, Rhondda Cynon Taff
2. Abertillery, Ebbw Vale, Blaenau Gwent
3. Caerphilly, Caerphilly
4. Church Village, Pontypridd, Rhondda Cynon Taff
5. Edwardsville, Pontypridd, Rhondda Cynon Taff
6. Ely, Rhiwbina, Cardiff
7. Gilfach Goch, Pontypridd, Rhondda Cynon Taff
8. Greenfield Terrace, Ebbw Vale, Blaenau Gwent
9. Treharris, Pontypridd, Rhondda Cynon Taff

List of freefone/lo-call providers

Freephone providers can route your 0800 number to your landline at a cost to you of as little as 3p a minute. You can also route your 0800 number to your mobile for more. Lo-call 0845 numbers are available from the following providers, which means that the caller only pays the cost of a local call. The cost to you is nothing! The reason for this is because the provider wants your volume of calls. There are even some numbers that you get paid per minute (0871 numbers), but only cost the caller a standard national call. Check out some of these providers:

Company Merchant Limited
Tel: (01527) 970 870
Website: www.telnos.co.uk

Crosby Communications
Tel: (0845) 200 6000
Email: customer.services@crosby.co.uk
Website: www.crosbycomms.co.uk

Dolphin
Tel: (0800) 634 8393
Email: customer.services@call08.com
Website: www.freephoneservices.co.uk

Efax
Tel: (0870) 711 3311
Email: sales@mail.efax.com
Website: www.efax.co.uk

Future Numbers
Tel: (0845) 130 1111
Website: www.future-numbers.co.uk

Global Telecom
Tel: (0800) 027 4717
Website: www.globaltelecomuk.com

Planet
Tel: (0845) 066 6666
Email: customer.services@planet-numbers.co.uk
Website: www.planet-numbers.co.uk

List of credit-checking agencies

Here is a list of credit-checking agencies. Some offer guarantees on the rent if the tenant defaults.

Homelet
Tel: (0845) 117 6000
Website: www.homeletuk.com

Letsure
Tel: (0870) 077 0880
Website: www.letsure.co.uk

Paragon
Tel: (0844) 800 3606
Website: www.paragon-plus.co.uk

The checks can be expensive, but if you put forward four prospective tenants under a guarantee scheme check, you could be spending nearly £300 – and this still doesn't mean that you would have found a tenant as all the tenants could have failed the credit check!

Guaranteed rent and maintenance contracts

Guaranteed rent can be obtained by one of three ways:

1. **Via an insurance contract.** This is where you pay a percentage of the rent to the insurer, typically three per cent, or a fixed fee to the insurer, to cover you against the tenant defaulting. The tenant has to be credit checked initially for a nominal fee, but from then on the rent is guaranteed. All the companies listed in the credit-checking agencies, above, provide this service.

2. **Obtaining a credit check for a one-off fee and then the rent is guaranteed if the tenant defaults.** All the companies listed in the credit-checking agencies, above, will do this for you.

3. **Getting a letting agent or institution to pay the rent direct.** Agents called Northwood Lettings (www.northwoodlettings.co.uk) and Your Move (www.your-move.co.uk) provide this service. These are growing chains of national estate agents who pay the rent directly to your bank account, even if the property is vacant. University institutions sometimes pay guaranteed rent, as they can then sublet your property to the students. It's worth contacting the university in

the area that you're thinking of buying. Councils are also paying guaranteed rent for asylum seekers or under the 'Empty Homes Scheme'. This is where the councils will even refurbish the property at no expense to yourself through a government grant in order to make your property tenantable. Schemes that I've found are www.carrick. gov.uk, (01872) 224 400, www.wealden.gov.uk, (01323) 443 313, and www.hastings.gov.uk, (01424) 781 305. I'm sure that there are many others.

If you want to obtain your own credit file, then you have to write to both Experian and Equifax. Ensure that you give them your full forename and surname, your date of birth and all addresses where you've resided during the past six years. Their addresses are:

Equifax Credit File Advice Centre
PO Box 1140
Bradford BD1 5US
Website: www.equifax.co.uk

Experian Consumer Help Service
PO Box 8000
Nottingham NG1 5GX
Website: www.experian.co.uk

Letting agents

I would suggest that you use only an Association of Residential Letting Agents (ARLA)-accredited member to collect your rent. Since the agent will be handling your money, you need to be covered against fraud, i.e. the agent running off with your money! If the agent commits any fraudulent acts, your money is fully guaranteed by ARLA. You don't even have to prove the fraud to get your money from ARLA.

Your local ARLA member can be found from www.arla.co.uk or by calling (0845) 345 5752.

Management software providers

I only really recommend one software provider, EZPZ Landlord. This is because there are few providers of this type of software and this one is the only one that is any good. You can download evaluation software from the website (www.ezpzsoftware.co.uk) for free! A fully working program for management of up to 20 properties costs £99 and if you want to have unlimited property records, it will cost you £299. The product details are as follows:

EZPZ Landlord – product details

EZPZ Landlord is a computer book-keeping system designed specifically to help landlords manage their properties. EZPZ Landlord has all the standard accounting features you would expect from a computerised book-keeping system:

- Sales ledger
- Purchase ledger
- Nominal ledger
- Bank reconciliation
- VAT analysis
- Automated entries
- Prepayments and accruals

with additional features including the calculation of rents and automated credit control for tenants. The system enables you to keep details of individual properties and tenants, and the links between them.

Properties

The property records form the main records of the system. Each property will have rent and tenancy records created for it. For example, a tenancy record will hold details of the type of tenancy, its duration and the tenant.

Each rent and tenancy record covers a period of time, so the system maintains a history of previous rent rates that have been in force, and the tenants who have occupied the property.

Rents may be based on any charging period such as weekly, calendar-monthly, quarterly, or you can define any non-standard period, and may be charged in advance or arrears.

Tenancies may be created for a property for any period and users may define their own tenancy types if unusual periods are involved. The Expiring Tenancies report shows properties for which the tenancy is due to expire.

Accommodation details may be recorded for each property and you can even store a picture within the property record. An inventory and schedule of condition may be created for each property. These may be used in periodic inspections of a property to assess possible damage by tenants.

Tenants

Each tenant's ledger shows what the tenant owes at any time. The automated credit control feature suggests what action to take based on how long rent charges have been overdue. Statements, reminders and final reminders can all be customised to your own requirements.

Tenancy agreements

Tenancy agreements may be printed for any tenancy with a few clicks of the mouse button. Agreements are created from a database of standard paragraphs that can be added, removed or customised, as you desire.

Reports

The system has a wealth of reports to offer, as you would expect from any book-keeping system. You can prepare a monthly profit and loss account, balance sheet and even carry out VAT analysis if you're VAT-registered.

Limitations of use

The demonstration version of the software limits the creation of properties to three. The registered version doesn't have this limitation. The number of records that may be created, using the registered version, is limited only by the amount of storage space you have.

System requirements

EZPZ Landlord was written using Microsoft Visual FoxPro V6.0 and is designed to run on any stand-alone PC and on any version of Windows including Windows 2000 Professional. To run EZPZ Landlord you'll need a minimum of:

- An IBM-compatible computer with a 486 66MHz processor (or higher)

- A mouse

- 16 MB RAM

- 10 MB free space on your hard drive

Support

Free help and support is available by telephone (office hours) and email, for the lifetime of the product.

Local newspapers

If you don't know the local newspaper in the area where you've just invested, there is a very good site that tells you: www.newspapersoc.org.uk. The Newspapers Society, (020) 7632 7400, will have details such as circulation figures, demographics and telephone numbers for you to place your advert.

List of auctioneers

Allsop & Co (Commercial)
27 Soho Square, London, W1D 3AY.
Tel: (020) 7437 6977
Website: www.allsop.co.uk

Allsop & Co (Residential)
Moreau House, 116 Brompton Road, Knightsbridge, London, SW3 1JJ.
Tel: (020) 7437 6977
Website: www.allsop.co.uk

Andrews & Robertson
75 Camberwell Church Street, London, SE5 8TU.
Tel: (020) 7703 4401
Email: auctions@a-r.co.uk
Website: www.a-r.co.uk

Athawes Son & Co.
203 High Street, Acton, London, W3 9DR.
Tel: (020) 8992 0056/0122
Email: mail@athawesauctioneers.co.uk
Website: www.athawesauctioneers.co.uk

Barnard Marcus
Auction Office, Commercial House, 64–66 Glenthorne Road, London, W6 0LR.
Tel: (020) 8741 9990/9001
Email: auctions.hammersmith@sequencehome.co.uk
Website: www.barnardmarcusauctions.co.uk

Countrywide Property Auctions
80–86 New London Road, Chelmsford, CM2 0PD.
Tel: (0870) 240 1140
Email: mlw@auctions.cwea.co.uk
Website: www.countrywidepropertyauctions.co.uk

Drivers & Norris
407–409 Holloway Road, London, N7 6HP.
Tel: (020) 7607 5001
Email: auction@drivers.co.uk
Website: www.drivers.co.uk

Erinaceous Auctions (Commercial)
10 Queen Anne Street, London, W1G 9LH.
Tel: (020) 7299 7300
Website: www.erinaceous.com

Erinaceous Auctions (Residential)
23 Brighton Road, South Croydon, CR2 6EA.
Tel: (020) 8649 7255
Website: www.erinaceous.com

FPD Savills
139 Sloane Street, London, SW1X 9AY.
Tel: (020) 7730 0822
Website: www.fpdsavills.co.uk

Halifax National Property Auctions
National Auction Division, 1st Floor, 158 Bramcote Lane, Wollaton, Nottingham, NG8 2QP.
Tel: (01773) 769 971
Website: www.halifaxauctions.co.uk

Keith Pattinson Ltd
210 High Street, Gosforth, Newcastle-upon-Tyne, Tyne & Wear, NE3 1HH.
Tel: (0845) 146 1582
Website: www.pattinson.co.uk

Nelson Bakewell
25, Sackville Street, London, W1S 3HQ.
Tel: (020) 7544 2000
Website: www.nelson-bakewell.com

Roy Pugh & Company
5 Lockside Office Park, Lockside Road, Preston, Lancashire, PR2 2YS.
Tel: (01772) 722 444
Email. auctions@pugh-company.co.uk
Website: www.pugh-company.co.uk

Strettons
Auction Office, Central House, 189–203 Hoe Street, London, E17 3SZ.
Tel: (020) 8520 8383
Email: auctions@strettons.co.uk
Website: www.strettons.co.uk

Ward & Partners
Christchurch House, Beaufort Court, Sir Thomas Longley Road, Medway
City Estate, Rochester, Kent, ME2 4FX.
Tel: (01634) 735 630
Email: auction@wardandpartners.co.uk
Website: www.wardandpartners.co.uk

Glossary

APR	Annual Percentage Rate. This rate is the true cost of borrowing. It takes into account all the fees in obtaining the loan, such as arrangement fees, the actual interest rate on the loan and when the payments are due for the duration of the loan. This avoids mortgage companies misleading the public by quoting a low initial interest rate for the start of the loan and then hitting them with a high interest rate after the initial period. That is why you see adverts for mortgages quoting an attractive initial interest rate and an APR rate. An APR rate has to be quoted in all adverts and publications by law.
ARLA	Association of Residential Letting Agents. A body that regulates letting agents for the letting agents who wish to subscribe to the body. They provide protection for both tenants and landlords.
Arrangement fees	Fees payable to lenders for arranging the mortgage. They can be added to the loan or be paid upon completion.
BOE	Bank of England Base Rate. This is the interest rate set by the Bank of England in conjunction with the government to control the economy. Mortgage rates are generally set around this figure.
Capital	This is the amount of money you've personally invested, i.e. not borrowed.

Capital appreciation	This is the difference between what you paid for the property and what the property is worth now.
Commission	This is a fee paid to agents based on a percentage of the rental income or selling cost for the services provided by the agent.
Deposit	This is the total money required to obtain the mortgage. This is based as a percentage of the purchase price of the property.
DSS	The Department of Social Security. The governmental agency that is responsible for paying out housing benefit to landlords.
Endowment mortgage	A mortgage where you pay the interest on the balance only and then take out an endowment policy to pay the balance of the mortgage at the end of the term of the mortgage. An endowment is a savings scheme where you contribute on a monthly basis and this contribution is invested on the stock market. There is no guarantee that at the end of the term the endowment policy will cover the balance of the mortgage balance.
Equity	The difference between the market value of the house and the borrowings taken out on it.
Exchange of contracts	At this point the buyer and seller are legally bound to transfer ownership. After this, completion occurs usually within one month when all the monies are exchanged.
Freehold	Ownership of a property without time constraint.
Gazumping	This is where the vendor accepts a higher offer from someone else, even though he has accepted an offer already. This is legal if the vendor hasn't exchanged contracts at the point he has accepted the new offer.
Gazundering	This is where the buyer places another offer lower to the original offer accepted by the vendor prior to exchange of contracts.
Gearing	Gearing an investment simply means borrowing to acquire the investment. The higher the gearing, the higher the borrowing.

Gross yield	This is the annual rental income expressed as a percentage of the total purchase price of the property.
Ground rent	A nominal amount, usually £50, payable to the freeholder due to the ownership of a leasehold.
Guarantor	A guarantor is liable for all debts unpaid by the borrower. A typical guarantor would be a parent of the borrower. So if the son defaults, the lender knows that it can chase the dad for the balance, as he is more likely to be able to pay.
Interest only mortgage	A mortgage where you only pay the interest of the amount borrowed and then settle the balance in full at the end of the mortgage term.
ISA mortgage	Like an endowment mortgage, but the saving scheme is an ISA (Individual Savings Account). This has various tax benefits, but there are restrictions on total contributions.
LIBOR	London Inter Bank Offered Rate. This is set and fixed quarterly on the first working day of March, June, September and December. It's the average of all the large banks' base rates.
LTV	Loan to value. The loan is expressed as a percentage of the purchase price or valuation. So a loan of £85,000 on a property costing £100,000 is an 85 per cent LTV loan.
Mortgage	A loan that is secured on the property. This means that you own the property, but if you default on the loan, the lender can order the property to be sold to recover its debt. Any surpluses arising from the sale are yours.
Negative equity	This is where the mortgage on the property exceeds the market value of the property. The amount it exceeds it by is the amount of negative equity.
Net yield	This is the annual profit expressed as a percentage of the total purchase price of the property. Profit being rental income less mortgage costs and repairs.

Payment in advance	This is where the tenant pays the rent at the start of the period.
Payment in arrears	This is where the tenant pays the rent at the end of the period.
Pension mortgage	Like an endowment mortgage, but the saving scheme is a pension. This has various tax benefits, but there are restrictions on total contributions and the borrower's age at the end of the term.
Profit	All incomes less all expenditure, excluding all asset sales and purchases.
Redemption penalty	The financial penalty that is liable if you were to repay the debt early in full.
Remortgage	This is where you already have a mortgage, but you wish to change lender. The new lender settles the debt to the existing lender. Remortgaging has two key features: 1. You can obtain a better interest rate (or a rate that suits you, e.g. fixed) than you're currently paying on your existing borrowings by sourcing the most suitable lender on the market. Your existing lender may be uncompetitive or unable to provide the type of mortgage you require. 2. You can raise finance on the increase of value of your property. So, for example, if you own a property that you purchased for £100,000 10 years ago with a £95,000 mortgage which is now worth £200,000, you can remortgage and access the £100,000 increase by getting a mortgage for say £190,000, releasing £95,000.
Repayment mortgage	A mortgage where you pay the interest and the capital over the duration of the mortgage. This type of mortgage ensures that you pay off the mortgage at the end of the term.
Repossession	Repossession occurs when the borrower defaults on the mortgage and the lender legally has to enforce the sale of the property to recover its debt.

Return	Same as gross yield.
Secured loan	The term secured means that the lender is 'secured' to get payment on the loan if the borrower defaults. The loan is only granted if you can supply sufficient security, typically being a house or car. If you default, the lender can repossess the security, sell it on the open market and recover its debt.
Service charge	The charge paid to service the property on which you have a lease. The service charge is a proportion of the total repairs and maintenance costs in the year.
Title deeds	Legal documents that show the legal ownership of the property.
Under offer	A property that has an offer accepted by the vendor, but the vendor and the purchaser haven't exchanged contracts.
Unsecured loan	A loan where no security has been offered by the borrower to the lender. The lender has only the courts to go to if the borrower defaults to enforce payment.

Index

H

I